THE
RESEARCH
PAPER
A Contemporary Approach
Second Edition

D1316211

THE
RESEARCH
PAPER
A Contemporary Approach
Second Edition

SHARON SORENSON

AMSCO SCHOOL PUBLICATIONS, INC.
315 Hudson Street
New York, NY 10013

As an English teacher and department chair in Indiana, SHARON SOREN-
SON has taught the research paper to over 1,000 students. She has also
taught at the University of Evansville and written nineteen books for students and teachers. She is presently a full-time writer and lecturer.

Consultant: JOANNE ARTZ, Reference Services Librarian at the
Rice Library, University of Southern Indiana

Cover Design: MERRILL HABER

Composition: COMPSET, INC.

When ordering this book, please specify:
Either **R 598 P** or **The Research Paper, Second Edition.**

Please visit our Web site at: www.amscopub.com

ISBN 978-1-56765-140-9 / *NYC Item* 56765-140-8
Copyright © 2006, 1999, 1994 by Amsco School Publications, Inc.

Printed in the United States of America

2 3 4 5 6 7 8 9 10   10 09 08 07

Acknowledgments

Writing a book like this requires not only the experience of having taught the research process to hundreds of students but also a treasure chest of ideas from fellow research teachers and fellow researchers. I received help and support from many generous people, but I feel especially grateful to Judy Hanefeldt at the Vanderburgh County Library for spending hours with me and my manuscript. The University of Southern Indiana Library staff also offered steady advice, especially Joanne Artz, Reference Services Librarian at USI's Rice Library. Mike Russ and Bob Hammonds extended their computer technology expertise. My sincere thanks to all.

My heartfelt appreciation goes to two special colleagues who shared with me their students' work and their own observations about teaching the research process. Susan J. Wolf, adjunct professor of English at University of Southern Indiana, and Shirley Everett, Master English teacher in the Evansville-Vanderburgh School Corporation, offered suggestions and extended support.

My new friends Terry Gish and Sarah Blaser have made a significant contribution to this book; I am indebted to them. As high school seniors, they shared their research papers as well as their research experiences. Their comments add a personal dimension to this book that other students will surely enjoy.

Preface

You have been assigned a research paper. Its due date is in what seems the distant future. The time between now and the due date will be very useful to you if you complete each necessary step, one at a time, until you have the finished product. Even the longest, most difficult task can be broken down into simple steps. All you need is time (which you have) and a good plan (which this book will give you). You will also have company as you work through each step. Terry and Sarah, two students whose research papers are included in the book, will share their experiences and help you avoid problems along the way.

In addition to their advice, Sarah and Terry share their completed papers with you. Terry's functions as a model for an assigned work of literature, Sarah's as a social issues topic of her own choice. Both papers use primary and secondary resources in their research, and both use the humanities style parenthetical form to document their research. Although both are evaluative papers, Terry's purpose is to compare and contrast, and Sarah's purpose is to show cause and effect. Each is accompanied by an analysis of content, organization, documentation, manuscript style, and formatting. In addition, Chapter 15 explains and models the science-style documentation form.

THE RESEARCH PAPER also focuses on the rapidly changing world of research. Technology affects not only how we find research materials but also how we put the information together. This book addresses the process of on-line research and also deals with documenting on-line sources. In addition, it acknowledges the role of technology in prewriting, writing, and revising while recognizing that various hardware/software combinations produce different capabilities.

In short, THE RESEARCH PAPER offers a dual approach:

1. the study and application of traditional research techniques
2. the implementation of modern technology

As you work, you will probably find that completing a research paper can be interesting (if not always fun), and you will learn a great deal about organizing your ideas and your time. These are the kinds of skills that can help you in many ways throughout your life. So, relax and enjoy the process as much as you can. (Some of it *is* fun.) After it's over, you will be left with a gratifying sense of accomplishment—and that is a very good feeling!

Contents

Choosing a Topic

During your years in school, you will probably write dozens of papers. Teachers and professors have a variety of reasons for assigning them: to test your ability to find material and present it in an organized manner, to test your understanding of a specific topic, to test your ability to apply some principle or theory to a specific situation. The paper is, indeed, a kind of test. From the student's point of view, however, writing a paper also teaches a great deal: you will learn how to locate information, how to select from among the many sources those most appropriate for your topic, how to analyze that material, and how to put it together so that readers will understand what you have learned about a new subject. To learn to write a successful paper is to take a giant step toward academic success, for the grade on a paper can sometimes be half the grade for a course.

The secret of creating a successful research paper is a three-pronged commitment:

1. *You must make a significant time commitment.* Unfortunately, there is no way to reduce the time needed to prepare a successful paper, so plan accordingly. A good time management plan, however, will keep you from wasting hours, and using time efficiently is almost the same as reducing it. This book includes a time management section in each chapter.

2. *You must make a commitment to work.* The task of completing a successful research paper is not overwhelming if you follow a step-by-step

plan. This book takes you through that plan. Remember, however, that there are no shortcuts to good papers, so do not plan to skip steps—or even to slight them.

3 *You must make a personal commitment.* You must become personally involved in your paper, researching and writing about something that interests you. Without that interest, your paper will lack spark, vitality, spirit, life. And no one—especially teachers and instructors—enjoys reading dull, drab papers. Guess what happens when they do. So this chapter helps you choose a good topic, because a topic that interests you and brings out your best work will also interest your readers and bring out their best responses.

In order to choose a good topic, you must first understand your purpose. What is this research paper supposed to accomplish? Is its purpose to report facts and statistics, reach a conclusion, solve a problem, relate opinions, evaluate, compare or contrast, or explain how or why? Is its purpose merely to prove that you can do research, organize the information, and present it in an interesting manner and in an acceptable form? Once you clearly identify the purpose, you can better choose an appropriate topic.

KINDS OF PAPERS

The term "research paper" is sometimes used interchangeably with expressions like "report," "library report," "term paper," or simply "paper." In spite of the fact that these expressions are sometimes used interchangeably, they do not always refer to the same kind of paper. Let's examine some of the kinds of papers you may be asked to write.

Report

A report, as the name suggests, reports what you have read or learned. It summarizes information that was usually gleaned from a single source—an article, chapter, or book. A report is objective and concerned only with facts: the training a meteorologist needs, how a radio works, the vehicles that carried people into space during the first 20 years of space exploration, what Benjamin Franklin's political life was about, the plot Herman Wouk developed in *War and Remembrance*. In other words, a report develops a topic but not a thesis. (More on thesis later.)

Factual Research Paper

A factual research paper is a more complicated kind of report. It summarizes information gleaned not just from one source, but from a series of resources, perhaps both print and nonprint, and both primary sources (firsthand materials, including someone's original words, like novels, interviews, and letters) and secondary sources (secondhand materials, including words about someone, like books and magazine and newspaper articles). The writer must merge the information from the various sources into one smooth, coherent product. It, too, deals with the facts about a given topic; it, too, develops a topic but not a thesis.

Evaluative Research Paper

An evaluative research paper relies on numerous references, often both primary and secondary sources, print and nonprint. Again, the writer must merge the information from the various sources into a smooth, coherent product; however, its content differs dramatically from that of a factual research paper. The evaluative paper goes beyond mere reporting. It may address solutions to a problem, determine causes or effects, formulate evidence to prove or disprove, compare or contrast, assess, analyze, or interpret. By presenting facts, figures, and opinions from both primary and secondary resources, the evaluative paper supports both a topic and a thesis statement. The result is that the reader gains a new point of view or sees information in a new light. Instead of reporting on the training a meteorologist needs, an evaluative research paper may compare the training a meteorologist needed in 1940 with what he or she needs many years later. Instead of reporting on the vehicles that carried people into space during the first 20 years of space exploration, an evaluative paper may attempt to prove the superiority of one vehicle over another. Instead of reporting what Benjamin Franklin's political life was about, an evaluative paper may analyze his writing style and how it may have affected his political career. Instead of reporting the plot Herman Wouk developed in *War and Remembrance*, an evaluative paper may compare the treatment of war in this novel with that in Wouk's earlier *Winds of War*.

An evaluative paper, as opposed to the objective report or factual paper, may also reach a conclusion that expresses an opinion. That point of view may explain support for a certain position or solution or declare a conclusion about some controversy. Obviously any support or concluding opinions must stem from research reported in the text.

Term Paper

The label "term paper" is a generic name for a paper written for a specific course during a specific semester—or term. "Term paper" can refer to a wide variety of papers. For instance, a term paper may be a writer's response to a piece of literature, a paper that presents the writer's opinion and uses no outside resources for support. For example, it could be an analysis of how F. Scott Fitzgerald develops the themes in *The Great Gatsby*. On the other hand, a term paper may be a full-blown factual or evaluative research paper requiring numerous resources. An example would be a comparison of what the critics have said about Fitzgerald's use of symbolism in *The Great Gatsby* followed by your own conclusions about the critics' analyses.

In other words, if you are assigned a "term paper," be sure to find out if you are to write a report, a factual or evaluative research paper, or a critical essay.

TECH TIP

A fair warning is in order: The world of research is fraught with danger. The most serious danger rests in a commonly mistaken idea: Some students think you just sit down at the computer, type in a few words, and all the information spills across your screen. Hardly. In fact, a major part of your work takes place before you ever turn on the machine.

But there's more danger. The Internet is filled with temptations to copy whole passages, string them together, and turn them in as your research paper. That's theft. It's called plagiarism. If you do this, you will certainly get an F on your paper, you may flunk the course, and you may even be expelled from school. That's *really* bad news. So be warned.

KINDS OF ASSIGNMENTS

When the time comes to write a research paper, you will be asked to meet certain criteria. One is length. Most assignments call for something between 1,000 and 2,000 words (a double-spaced printed page is about 250 words and Sarah's model paper, found in Chapter 14, runs about 1,700 words). You will also face one of three situations: the topic will be assigned, the general subject area will be assigned, or neither will be assigned—you will be given free rein to select a topic. In any case, your work should show original thought. Completing the assignment is more than just researching and writing; it is also an exercise in independent thinking.

Topic Assigned

If the topic is assigned, chances are that you are being evaluated on your ability to do thorough research on a specific topic and to put the resulting information together into a clearly organized, accurately presented paper. Part of the "test" is to see whether you can develop a paper that distinguishes you from the rest of your classmates. Thus, even with an assigned topic, you must still narrow the focus or determine the approach you will take. For instance, if your assigned topic is "The Effects of Sun on Humans," you may decide to focus on research supporting the theory that harmful sun rays can cause skin cancer. You may decide to focus on research that suggests the sun ages skin and makes wrinkles form early in life. You may take the approach that, given the sun's harmful effects, people can follow certain steps to protect themselves.

General Subject Area Assigned

If the general subject area is assigned, you still have other decisions to make about a topic. Within the general subject area assigned, you must select a specific, narrowed topic as well as a specific focus. For instance, if your social science teacher asks for a research paper dealing with some aspect of the Vietnam War, you must determine a specific emphasis. Will you limit your research to the media's treatment of the first year of the war? To the antiwar demonstrations? To the still-missing prisoners of war? To the role of the war during a presidential election campaign? To the after-war conditions of Vietnamese civilians? To Vietnam veterans' current reactions to the war?

Wherever possible, turn an assigned general topic into an opportunity to pursue personal interests. For instance, a student interested in the protection of rain forests may choose to turn a paper about the Vietnam War into an analysis of the long-term effects of the wartime defoliation of forests. Another student, concerned about abandoned children, may turn the paper into an examination of what happened to the Amerasian children fathered by American soldiers during the war.

Topic Unassigned

If you have free rein in choosing your topic, you must select not only the general subject but must also narrow the topic. Where do you look for ideas?

TECH TIP

Certain CD-ROM writing tutorials include inspirations, graphic organizers, and other topic-generating tools. Use them!

If you do not have access to such tools, use your word processing software to write lists. Write as fast as you can, letting ideas flow. Print a copy and put it away for 24 hours. Then, reread your lists and let your mind add new ideas, new reactions, new relationships. The exercise should help you narrow your topic.

WARNING: Always make backup files. To risk a malfunctioning computer or the mysterious loss of material to the airwaves is to risk hours of time lost.

CRITICAL THINKING HINT

When you are struggling to think of topics, put your brain in gear and let go. Think of relationships, causes, effects, comparisons, contrasts, results, and solutions. Think about why, how, and when. Let ideas flow.

SOURCES FOR TOPICS

Sources for topics are limitless, but let's consider several of the most likely.

Daily Media

Newspapers and magazines print or publish electronically articles of current concern. Radio and television have no shortage of newscasts, news analyses, and news commentaries. While you must avoid a topic too new to have adequate resources available, other issues are ongoing and have been for many years. Read or listen "between the lines." Assume a questioning attitude. What issues or problems underlie the present news item? For instance, if a television commentary deals with urban crime, you may wonder which cities have the highest crime rates and how they are trying to deal with the problem. That may lead you to think about urban poverty, the judicial system, and drug rehabilitation programs. Think. Make the mental connections.

General Schoolwork

Class work or reading assignments often suggest suitable research topics. For instance, after studying in physics class the effect of the moon on tides, you may decide to investigate the probability that the moon exerts enough pull on the earth to have other effects. You wonder what they are. Think critically. Ask yourself the underlying questions.

General Conversation

As you talk on a daily basis with friends, neighbors, and family, keep your ears open for issues that pop into conversations. When your friend complains about his working hours, maybe you decide to check into laws affecting conditions for workers under age 18. When your neighbor talks about her lawn mower never wanting to start, maybe you decide to examine what consumer protection groups do and their results. When your father talks about the potential for an upcoming labor strike, maybe you decide to research the role of unions on consumer prices. Be an active thinker. Look for causes, effects, conditions, and results.

Personal Interests

Since your topic should be interesting to you, think about a personal fascination that might suggest a topic. If your interest is music, consider the impact one composer has had on another or the role one musician has played in the development of jazz. If your current job is in the produce section of the local grocery, consider the problems with imported produce: it is not grown under the same stringent laws restricting toxic pesticides and herbicides as the produce grown in the United States. If you plan to be an electrical engineer, consider the rapidly changing field of electronics and what that means to career planning. Think about how and why. Think about connections.

Your Own Mind

The best source of topics is your own active mind. As you read and listen, become an active thinker. Make connections. Ask yourself questions. Wonder why or how. Think in comparisons or contrasts. Question causes or effects. Suppose changes. Consider alternatives. Contemplate the past or the future. Seek answers.

TECH TIP

Once you have determined a general area of interest for your topic, with your teacher's permission, try a *keyword search* on the World Wide Web to help you find a topic. Later, you'll learn more about keyword searches and how to get the best results.

If you do a keyword search at this point, look only at the resulting list of Web *sites*. Just *surf*, or browse; don't search. Don't waste time going to the sites themselves. Instead, use the results to stimulate your thinking.

Once you've seen the list of sites that a basic keyword search turns up, you'll find subtopics and related ideas that will help you brainstorm. In other words, you're using the Web only as a tool to put your brain in gear!

CHARACTERISTICS OF GOOD TOPICS

When choosing a topic for a research paper, select one that has the following characteristics:

1 *Interesting* You will be working closely with this topic for an extended time, so choosing a topic that interests you will make your task more palatable. On the other hand, avoid a topic with which you are already thoroughly knowledgeable. It is no fun researching the distinguishing characteristics of Confederate notes if you already know all about the currency. Choose a subject that so interests you that you want to learn more about it.

2 *Manageable* A topic is unmanageable when: (a) you must wade through hundreds of periodical and book references to find information and (b) you cannot develop adequate support within the assigned length of the paper.

3 *Available* You must choose a topic that is available for research, for which resources are obtainable. If you cannot find material on your topic, either because available resources are limited or because the topic is too narrow, you cannot successfully complete a paper.

4 *Worthwhile* Whether or not a paper is worthwhile is, of course, a value judgment; but a topic of doubtful worth will likely earn a doubtful grade. So what do we mean by worthwhile? Your paper must say something of substance. To write a research paper that merely outlines the history of space exploration lacks the impact of a paper that analyzes the struggle for success in space exploration. Do yourself—and your reader—a favor by dealing with a subject that matters.

5 *Original* Recounting Abraham Lincoln's biography lacks original thought, but you can show original ideas by focusing on how a single aspect of his life, like the books he read as a boy, seems to have influenced his later political decisions.

Finally, a good topic does not have the following characteristics of poor topics.

CHARACTERISTICS OF POOR TOPICS

As you strive for the ideal topic, keep in mind the following characteristics of poor research topics. In general, avoid topics that fall into one of the following categories:

1 *Too broad* Students' most common mistake is choosing a topic that is too broad. Perhaps they are afraid they cannot find adequate material. Perhaps 1,000 or 1,500 words sounds like an impossible length (really only about six or seven typewritten pages). Whatever the cause, avoid that trap yourself. If your subject is too broad, you will be unable to develop the topic adequately.

How will you know if a topic is too broad? You may find entire books on your subject, a sure indication that you have tackled too much. You may find dozens of subheadings in online searches or catalogs, another sure sign of a too-broad topic.

Consider these broad topics: the Great Wall of China, Salem Witchcraft Trials, the Ice Age, Hieroglyphics—all much too broad for an average 1,500-word paper. All, however, can be narrowed: what tourists experience when they visit the Great Wall of China, the effect of the Salem witchcraft trials on present-day Salem, the role of the Ice Age in the formation of the Great Lakes, how original Egyptian hieroglyphics are protected.

CRITICAL THINKING HINT

To narrow a topic, ask yourself questions that help you think critically. Start with the 5 W's: who? what? why? when? and where? If those questions do not help you narrow your topic sufficiently, ask the analytical questions: How did this come to be? What are the causes? What are the results? What happens next? How does this compare? How does this contrast? What is the value? These questions will help you think through your topic. Then let your mind make connections.

2 *Too narrow* If your subject is too narrow, you will be unable to find adequate sources for your research. Unfortunately, when some students say they "can't find anything" about a subject, the problem may not be a too-narrow topic but the students' lack of experience in digging up references. To use research facilities effectively, you probably will not look up your specific topic, but rather you will look up a general topic and find specifics in subheadings or in chapter or index entries.

How do you know if a topic is too narrow? Consider these topics: the queen honeybee's role in the hive, metric cooking conversions, temperature extremes in the United States, and foreign car sales are all too narrow for a reasonable paper. Most of these topics can be reported in a few sentences or even in a single chart. On the other hand, the topics can be easily expanded: how honeybees' division of labor works, the complexity of national metric conversion, causes for temperature variations, the impact of foreign car sales on domestic production.

3 *Too trivial* A topic that is too trivial lacks worth. Too trivial is not the same as too narrow. For instance, if you decide to write about the process of developing photographic prints from a CD file, you have chosen a topic that is broad enough, but it is trivial. How will you know? Every source you pick up will explain the process in the same way. Likewise, if you write about how to obey the laws of the road, every driver's manual you read will say the same thing. Remember, a good research paper cannot come from a single source.

4 *Too subjective* A subjective topic is one that is biased or personal and, because of that bias, it also lacks the objectivity of a so-called "disinterested party." Preferably, you should choose a topic in which you can be a disinterested party. Every writer, of course, has personal opinions, and they often show through an otherwise objective piece of writing. However, choosing a research topic that reflects primarily personal opinion may result in a paper that you are unable to support with facts and statistics. Ideally, the process of writing a research paper—especially the research process itself—may help formulate an opinion. It is unwise, however, to begin with a prejudice you hope to prove. For instance, if you set out to write a research paper about congressional terms in office and you are already firmly convinced that terms should be limited to six years, your opinion will influence your selection of materials for your paper and cause you to lose objectivity. Unless your assigned purpose is to write a persuasive paper, avoid such subjective choices. Remember, a research paper cannot rely on personal opinion alone. Your supporting details must come from your research, primary or secondary, and those details should be used objectively.

5 *Too controversial* While many topics deal with some degree of controversy, to address a topic whose issues are hotly contested is to risk the chance of getting bogged down in the arguments. Most research papers are objective, not subjective; so to write about a highly controversial topic usually results in becoming personally involved in the controversy. Objectivity vanishes.

6 *Too familiar* While you may choose a topic that already interests you, avoid a topic about which you are so knowledgeable that you will gain no further insights as you do your research. Boredom results. Choose a topic that maintains your curiosity.

7 *Too technical* A topic too technical for your best friend may not be too technical for you. If you already have a working knowledge of how supplemental hormones affect the milk production of dairy cows, a topic addressing that issue may not be too technical for you. On the other hand, if you have never set foot on a dairy farm, you will be reading something akin to a foreign language as you do your research. Avoid trying to learn a technical language while at the same time trying to construct a successful research paper.

8 *Too factual* If your topic calls for nothing more than the recitation of facts, you have a poor topic. A biography of Thomas Jefferson, for instance, would recite facts. On the other hand, if you are particularly interested in Jefferson, you can choose a better focus. For instance, you could analyze the impact Jefferson had on some phase of early American politics.

9 *Too new* A late-breaking news item, no matter how interesting, will be an inappropriate topic. You will be unable to find sufficient research material to support your thesis.

10 *Too regional* If you live in Colorado and want to research the economic impact of the Amish in southeastern Minnesota, you will no doubt have trouble finding such regional information. On the other hand, if you live in Harmony, Minnesota, you may find both primary and secondary research materials readily available.

Once you have selected a topic that meets the above criteria, try phrasing it as a question. A good topic will take the form of a question, and the question becomes the guide for your research. For example, Renee phrased her topic in this research question: What elements are necessary in a landfill design to protect future generations? This question will guide her research. Later, the answer to the research question becomes the thesis statement or controlling idea for her paper. Thus, as you do your research, the topic (as expressed by your research question) does not change, but the thesis statement (the answer to the question) most certainly can change.

As a thinking human being, you need room to reach your own conclusions after you have done all the research. Your topic should let you do that—and report your conclusions. Remember, the best topics allow for judgment, not the simple reporting of facts.

SUGGESTIONS FOR GENERAL TOPICS

The following broad areas may help you make connections, ask questions, wonder how, or question why. Your thinking will help you narrow the broad areas into something suitable as a research topic.

Social Sciences: agriculture, political movements, battles, political or religious leaders, feminism, civil rights, summit conferences, Underground Railroad, carpetbaggers, media influence on elections, origin of democracy, economic impact, psychological study, cartography

Environment: landfills, toxic dumps, national lands, timber harvesting, recycling, wetlands, air and water pollution, endangered species, ozone layer, acid rain studies, greenhouse effect, environmental controls, EPA, pesticides, oil spills

Health: research funding, national health care, eating for good health, insurance, pesticides and herbicides, ethical and moral issues, sports medicine, exercise, selecting a doctor, cost control, transplants, artificial limbs or organs

Science and Technology: impact on education and the workplace, impact on home and daily life, electromagnetic fields, strip mine land reclamation, wildlife habitat, television's influence, robotics, fuel-efficient automobiles, space travel, Martian exploration

Home and Family: day care, early childhood education, home safety, cross-cultural education, school choice, single-parent families, latchkey children, home ownership, care of elderly, adoption, changing roles of men and women, care givers

Business: work incentives, employee-owned industry, cottage industries, family and corporate farms, investments, flexible work hours, changing assembly lines, robotics, communication changes, transportation, infrastructures

Music: composers, scores, instruments, lyrics, performers, audiences, types (jazz, rock, country, classical), recording facilities, Internet access, piracy

Entertainment: sports (injuries, recruitment, competition, role models, spectator sports), theater (changing, technical aspects, behind-the-scenes techniques, directing, musicals, cost), film (casting, competition for movie theaters, video, copyright controversy), television, stage vs. screen

Literature: an author, a single work, two authors or two works (compared or contrasted), a metaphor or symbol, universal or common themes, imagery, style, applied to daily life, reflection of author's life or historical period

A Model for Choosing Topics

The following chart models the selection of topics from a variety of cross-curricular general subject areas.

General subject:	civil rights
Unsuitable topics:	civil rights movement in the 1960s (too broad)
	my father's activities (too subjective)
Suitable topic:	What leadership role did Martin Luther King take during the early civil rights protest?
General subject:	any artist
Unsuitable topics:	Rembrandt (too broad)
	Andrew Wyeth as a child (too narrow)
Suitable topic:	What common techniques appear in five key works by Andrew Wyeth?
General subject:	any author studied in the English literature survey class
Unsuitable topics:	Tennyson as an author (too broad)
	Tennyson's education (too trivial)
Suitable topic:	What recurring symbols appear in Tennyson's work?
General subject:	any contemporary science issue
Unsuitable topics:	protecting the environment (too broad)
	designing coal-fired generators that use high-sulfur coal (too technical)
Suitable topic:	What effects will result from using gas-powered generators?

General subject:	historical causes of bankruptcy
Unsuitable topics:	causes of bankruptcy (too broad)
	causes of personal bankruptcy during 1929 (too trivial)
Suitable topic:	What national, local, and personal economic conditions caused John James Audubon to go to debtor's prison?
General subject:	an economic law or principle
Unsuitable topics:	how the law of supply and demand affects the economy (too broad)
	how the law of supply and demand affects my wages (too subjective)
Suitable topic:	How does the law of supply and demand affect the price of automobiles?

Time Management Guidelines

Choosing the right topic will make or break your research paper. While this first step is crucial, do not waste time here using the excuse, "I can't think of anything." If you cannot think of anything, you are not thinking. Ideas are everywhere. Get busy. Read. Talk to people. Think. Sit and write for at least 30 minutes about things that interest you.

To fall behind at this point is deadly. Accept the fact that your life will always be governed by deadlines, and the research paper is just one small part of all those deadlines.

How much time can you spend selecting a topic? That depends on how much time you have to complete the entire writing process. Use this general guideline:

Number of weeks until final paper is due	Number of days available to select a topic
10	4
8	3
6	2
4	1

TWO STUDENTS' PROGRESS

We will be following two students as they work their way from choosing the topic through completing the final paper. Sarah and Terry face very different kinds of assignments, so perhaps their experiences will help you meet your own assignment. You will hear from both of them in each chapter.

Sarah

My paper was for my senior English class. Our teacher gave us the choice of almost any topic that interested us. The assignment was to prepare an evaluative research paper of 1,500–2,000 words and incorporate in it a variety of resources, both primary and secondary. So I wanted a topic for which I could find all kinds of references—periodicals, books, pamphlets, and Internet sources. And part of the assignment required that I do at least one personal interview.

Earlier I had read that a company chose to build a plant in a location where the fewest acres of wetlands would be affected, so I started wondering what wetlands really are and why they matter. That was my general topic, but I knew it was too broad. To help me think, I started writing a list of questions:

> What are wetlands?
> Why are wetlands getting attention from the environmentalists and the news media?
> Why not just fill in the wetlands to get rid of the mosquitoes and use the land to farm or build houses?
> What lives in wetlands? What kinds of plants and animals? Are they important?
> What happens if we get rid of wetlands?

My teacher said that often a good topic can be worded as a question, and I could certainly say I had lots of questions!

Terry

My class had been reading John Steinbeck's *The Grapes of Wrath*, so the teacher assigned an evaluative research paper in which we were to respond to the novel. The teacher said we should look for "a truth or insight into life as expressed in this novel." We were to write a 600- to 1,000-word paper and use six references: two historical sources, two literary critiques, one personal interview, and, of course, the novel itself. The personal interview was to be with someone who lived during the Depression, and the questions asked were to seek out experiences that compare with or contradict those of the Joads, the main characters in the novel. As our teacher said, "Decide on something you learned from the novel and your other resources and then write a thesis statement." So my topic was assigned, and I just had to narrow the focus. Right away I began thinking about my grandfather who lived through the Great Depression.

TIPS AND TRAPS

Sarah and Terry offer these suggestions for avoiding typical traps:

Don't choose a topic just because a friend does. You'll be competing for materials and getting in each other's way as deadlines draw near.

Don't choose a topic just because you think you have a couple of books at home on that topic and you can save yourself some work at the library. And don't choose a topic just because a keyword search on the Web gave you 9,000 hits! You'll be lulled into a false sense of security.

If your topic is assigned, remember that everyone else in the class has the same assignment. So focus your paper creatively. Try to make it something different from what everybody else is doing. You'll be more successful.

CHECKLIST FOR CHOOSING A TOPIC

Use the following checklist to judge your topic choices. A good topic should earn an honest "yes" to each of these questions.

1. Am I interested in this topic?
2. Am I avoiding a topic with which I am already thoroughly familiar?
3. Have I narrowed the topic sufficiently?
4. Have I avoided a topic that is too technical for my personal background?
5. Will I be able to find adequate resources for this topic?
6. Is this topic worthwhile?
7. Does this topic avoid undue controversy that may bog me down?
8. Does this topic rely primarily on objective rather than subjective material?

9. Does this topic address more than a recitation of facts?
10. Does this topic meet the requirements of the assignment?
11. Will this topic permit me to write a paper that shows original thought?
12. Can I word this topic as a question?

EXERCISES

Exercise A: *Choosing Suitable Topics*

Directions: Study the following list of topics. Decide which are suitable for a research paper of about 1,000 words. For unsuitable topics, explain or discuss why each is not satisfactory and then alter each to make it satisfactory.

1. Time Management for Students
2. Population Increase in the United States
3. Defense Spending
4. Potential Health Problems for Joggers
5. Advantages of Athletics
6. Use of Handwriting Analysis in Hiring Practices
7. Voters' Responsibilities
8. Effects of Limiting Political Terms in Office
9. Effects of Advertising
10. Crime in Montana
11. Furniture Design
12. Frank Lloyd Wright's Contributions to Architecture
13. "Prairie School" Architecture
14. How to Play a Carillon
15. Development of the Interstate Highway System
16. Automobile Exhaust Emissions' Effect on the Ozone Layer
17. Major Pollutants to the World's Atmosphere
18. The Effect of Labor Unions on Consumer Prices
19. Training to Be a Super Athlete
20. How I Fight Peer Pressure

Exercise B: *Narrowing Broad Topics*

Directions: All of the following topics are too broad. Narrow each so that it is suitable for a 1,000-word research paper.

1. Subliminal Advertising
2. Ancient Cosmetics

3. Kinds of Canoes
4. How to Audition
5. Characteristics of Successful Artists
6. Anesthetics
7. The John Birch Society
8. Pythagoras
9. Chesapeake Bay
10. World Languages

Doing the Preliminary Work

2

At this point, we will make the following assumptions:

- You have chosen or been assigned a general topic.
- You may or may not have narrowed the topic.
- You may or may not have determined your research question.
- You have not yet written a thesis statement.

With these assumptions in mind, this chapter will prepare you for the actual research task. Before you rush headlong into the research, you should complete two steps:

1 *Do some preliminary reading.* The preliminary reading will help you narrow your general topic. If the topic is unassigned or if you have been assigned only a general subject area, the preliminary reading will also clarify your purpose and research question.

2 *Prepare a working outline.* The working outline will guide your research and save you hours of wasted effort. Although the working outline changes as the research progresses, it nevertheless serves as a guide for your work.

This chapter helps you complete these two steps.

PRELIMINARY READING

In order to narrow your general topic and work toward a thesis statement, you will need to do some preliminary research. In fact, it may be more accurate if we do not call your work at this stage "research," but instead call it "reading"—general (or preliminary) reading. This initial reading is something like exploring a new vacation spot in order to find out where you want to spend the bulk of your time.

Remember that preliminary reading should be limited to general sources that address your broad topic in a summary-like manner, and it should be done quickly, without taking notes.

Putting the Internet in Perspective

You may be surprised to learn that going to the Web is not the first step in doing your research.

The important thing to remember is this: When you start brainstorming and when you start *browsing* the *Web* depend on your topic. How so? Well, say your assignment is a really broad and well-known topic, like the death penalty. If so, you can brainstorm to come up with ideas for your focused topic. On the other hand, maybe you've been given a topic about which you know nothing. In this case, you may need to do some initial browsing on the Web. Of course, it's rare that you're be assigned a topic about which you know absolutely nothing. Most research projects are related to what you've been studying in class. So, for the most part, you'll brainstorm first and hit the Web later.

TECH TIP

When students jump immediately onto the Web to gather information (which is different from browsing to explore topic ideas), they omit a major part of the prewriting process. Remember that prewriting includes narrowing the topic and preparing a tentative plan. Without a narrowed topic and tentative plan, when faced with the glut of information on the 20,000 sites a keyword search turns up, you'd be totally lost. The usual reaction of many students is to check out the first two or three sites and write about what they find. Sorry, but that's not what research is all about.

 Searching for general references online is not the same as searching the Web. Many libraries subscribe to online databases. These may include general references like encyclopedias as well as full-text magazines and newspapers. All of these are considered general reading. We'll save discussions of Web research for a little later.

Finding General References

Most students have reasonable success doing preliminary research in a general or specialized encyclopedia. The most widely used general encyclopedias include the five listed below. Most of them are available electronically if your local library purchases the service.

> *World Book Encyclopedia*—a general, usually simplified reference
> *Collier's Encyclopedia*—a good supplement for high school and college curricula
> *Encyclopædia Britannica*—a good comprehensive reference; includes three parts: the *Propædia*, which serves as an outline and topical guide to the *Macropædia*; the *Macropædia*, which includes comprehensive, sometimes book-length, articles; and the *Micropædia*, which includes shorter articles but is *not* a short version of the *Macropædia*
> *The Encyclopedia Americana*—a comprehensive reference that is also especially good for science and technology
> *The Columbia Encyclopedia*—a one-volume encyclopedia with only the sketchiest entries but includes excellent bibliographies

If your topic is too specialized for the general reference sources, you may need to refer to a special encyclopedia like the *Encyclopedia of Social Sciences*, the *Jewish Encyclopedia*, or the *Encyclopedia of World Literature in the 20th Century*.

Other researchers have better success browsing in a general textbook. For instance, reading about Hawaii in a geography book will produce different ideas than will reading about it in a history book. Consider general textbooks in curricular areas that interest you: earth science, general business, economics, physics, woodworking, sociology, chemistry, accounting, business law, electronics, psychology.

These general references help you get key terms, dates, names, and a general framework before going to the catalog or indexes. At the same time, you'll find direction in narrowing your topic.

Using the General Reference

How do you use these general references? Look up your general topic and then read for ideas. Let's follow four students as they read.

Chin is interested in theater architecture. He looked up "Theater Architecture" in *The Encyclopedia Americana* and found the following general headings:

> Theater of the Ancient World
> Theater of the Renaissance
> Effect of Scenery Innovations
> Baroque and Rococo Theater
> Theater in America
> Nineteenth-Century Revolution
> Modern Playhouse

Since Chin hopes to seek a career in theater, working backstage, he was most attracted to the category "Effect of Scenery Innovations." As he read, he discovered that the Italians first introduced elaborate scenery changes and that one Italian, Giacomo Torelli, relocated in France where he introduced machines to move scenery. As Chin began making connections with what he was reading, he wondered if he could develop a paper that compares Torelli's work with contemporary stage equipment. He wondered how many of Torelli's ideas are still in use.

Connie has read a great deal about her cultural background and has recently become interested in pictography. One sentence in an article on pictography in the *Encyclopædia Britannica Micropædia* attracted her attention: "Various North American Indian tribes used pictographs as ideograms (a pictograph that stands for an individual idea) and as memory aids." She wondered if she could develop a paper that lets her combine photographs she has of area pictographs with research that will help her understand whether these were used as ideograms or as memory aids.

Carlos is interested in the migration patterns of animals. When he looked up "Migration, Animal" in the *Macropædia*, he found five general headings:

> Survey of Migrations in Animals
> Navigation and Orientation
> Physiological Stimulus of Migration
> Origin and Evolution of Migration
> Ecological Significance of Migration

Although he skimmed the entire article, he was struck by an example of a Manx shearwater that flew 3,050 miles (4,900 kilometers) from Massachusetts to Britain in 12 1/2 days. He was interested in how a bird could fly so far. In the section headed "Navigation and Orientation," Carlos found information about homing experiments and the birds' use of celestial navigation. He wondered if wet and dry seasons affected the birds' need to migrate, if prevailing winds affected them, and why birds seem to flock together during migration. He wondered if he could do a paper that explains how a single species migrates without getting lost, maybe narrowing that even further to climatic effects on migration. He noted, too, that the bibliography list at the end of the article included four books specifically addressing bird migrations.

Beth took a different approach. She has been interested in recent media comments about the success of Japanese business. Feeling poorly informed about Japan in general, she thumbed through a geography textbook and found, in a chapter about Japan, the following headings:

> Topography and Climate
> Resources
> Agricultural Efficiency
> Urban Industrial Core
> Industrialization after the War
> Manufacturing and Trade
> Life in Japan

Beth's attention focused on two sentences in the section on manufacturing: "For some Japanese workers, taking a job is like joining a family. They expect to go on working for that same company until they retire." She wondered how employers treated employees in order to earn that kind of loyalty and if this was still true. If it has changed, what caused it to do so? Then she read that Japan produced tremendous quantities of steel, automobiles, and computers. She wondered how Japan, a tiny country compared with the United States, could produce so much. What is there about the Japanese work ethic that gives them such success? Maybe her paper could compare the Japanese working conditions with those in the United States.

CRITICAL THINKING HINT

Think about your topic and write down exactly what you want to know about it. You should answer these questions:

1. What is my narrowed topic (written in the form of a question)?
2. What do I already know about my topic?
3. What do I want to learn about my topic?
4. Where can I find out what I need to learn about my topic?

You can put all this into a simple chart, like this.

General Topic: Cavity-Nesting Birds

Narrowed Topic: How do nonnative house sparrows and European starlings threaten native cavity-nesting birds?

The third column will guide your research.

K (What Do I Know?)	W (What Do I Want to Know?)	L (What Did I Learn?)
House sparrows and European starlings are not native birds.	Where did they come from? Why are they here?	
Some native birds nest in cavities.	Which native birds need nest cavities? What kinds of cavities do they need? Where must these cavities be located—high, low—or does it matter?	
House sparrows and European starlings take some of the same nest cavities that native birds want.	Which native birds are most affected? What are the results? How can native birds overcome this threat?	

STATING THE PURPOSE

After your preliminary reading, you can narrow your topic (if you haven't already) and clarify the purpose of your paper. For example, Chin worded his topic in this research question: How have Giacomo Torelli's stage ideas influenced modern theater? The purpose of his paper will be to show which of Torelli's inventions have evolved into present backstage machinery. His thesis statement will answer his research question. He will write his thesis statement after he completes his research.

Connie's topic is similarly worded: What characteristics distinguish ideogram pictographs from memory aids? The purpose of her paper will be to identify the two kinds of pictographs by comparing and contrasting their characteristics and to use photographs to clarify the identification. Her thesis statement will answer her research question.

Carlos phrased his research question as follows: How does the climate affect the migratory patterns of Canada geese? The purpose of his paper will be to find out how weather conditions, like storms or drought, affect the Canada geese's ability to find their way during migration. His thesis statement will answer his research question.

Finally, Beth's research question is worded this way: How do Japanese working conditions compare with those in the United States? The purpose of her paper will be to analyze why Japanese workers, as contrasted with American workers, more often stay with the same company until they retire. Like the others, her thesis statement will answer her research question.

WORKING OUTLINE

When you have narrowed your topic and clarified your purpose, you are ready to write your working outline. A working outline is what its name suggests: a preliminary outline that guides your work. Too early to write an outline, you say? No! If you do not map out a plan for your paper—and your work—before you begin doing research, you will haul home useless references, read unnecessary volumes, browse too many useless Web sites, and still find yourself without adequate material to support key ideas. Although you were advised in Chapter 1 that you must make a major time commitment to this project, you certainly do not want to waste time or spend more than necessary. To work effectively, then, write the working outline before you head to the library.

TECH TIP

Some writing software packages include prewriting activities, like idea webs, cluster maps, and brainstorming exercises. Although many programs lack the depth needed for

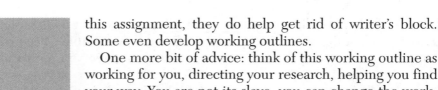

this assignment, they do help get rid of writer's block. Some even develop working outlines.

One more bit of advice: think of this working outline as working for you, directing your research, helping you find your way. You are not its slave; you can change the working outline as your reading suggests.

So how do you create this outline when you have read only a little? There are some logical steps to follow.

CRITICAL THINKING HINT

Writing the preliminary outline is a deductive thinking process. You have a general topic; it needs specific supporting details. So think deductively. What specific details explain this big, general topic? Try using a concept web like the one Sarah shares later, or try using a list. Both approaches will help you think deductively.

Let's try the list approach here. First, list questions that your paper needs to answer. For instance, assume you are interested in the general topic of laser technology. Your preliminary reading has made you curious about the effects of laser technology on surgery. You have decided your purpose will be to examine the effects of laser technology on general surgical procedures. As a result, you generate a list of the following questions:

1. Does laser technology speed surgery?
2. How do doctors decide when to use it?
3. Is the technology readily available?
4. What special facilities are necessary?
5. Are most doctors trained to do laser surgery?
6. Does it speed recovery?
7. Is it better for some surgeries than others?
8. Does it cost more than traditional surgery?
9. What dangers accompany laser surgery?
10. Do problems recur after laser surgery?
11. What damage can laser surgery cause?
12. Are there side effects from it?
13. What (if any) are the psychological problems before laser surgery?
14. Psychological effects afterward?
15. Length of hospital stay?

Second, from this list of questions you will generate a working outline. How? Think of the questions as main headings in your outline. The problem, of course, is that no outline needs 15 headings, so you must think through the questions. You will soon see that some topics overlap, some are related to one another, and some may be discarded, replaced, or altered. When you finish that thought process, you will have a preliminary outline.

Let's think through the development of a specific preliminary outline for the above questions to see how the process works.

First, notice that many of the questions concern when laser surgery is possible (questions 3, 4, and 5) or appropriate (questions 1, 2, and 7). Those questions fit together logically, so they can make up one heading, perhaps with two subheadings. Several questions (9, 11, and 12) deal with potential problems, so logically those three fit together into another heading. Other questions (6, 8, 10, and 15) address direct and indirect costs. The psychological factors (questions 13 and 14) seem to be another aspect of recovery.

Where does that leave the outline?

I. Elements for success
    A. Medical facilities (questions 3, 4, and 5)
    B. Patient condition (questions 1, 2, and 7)
II. Potential for problems (questions 9, 11, and 12)
III. Cost to patient
    A. Direct
        1. Surgery (question 8)
        2. Hospital stay (question 15)
    B. Indirect
        1. Recovery time (questions 6 and 10)
        2. Psychological impact (questions 13 and 14)

Is this a final outline? By no means. The outline will not be final until the paper is finished. Is this outline satisfactory for a working outline? Absolutely. It will guide your research. If this outline needs to be changed, when will the changes be made? The answer is, whenever you see the need to change—while you are reading, while you are thinking through the organization, while you are writing, while you are revising. By reminding you which specific topics your research must address, the working outline will save you hours of useless reading and keep you and your paper on target.

TIME MANAGEMENT GUIDELINES

The following two guidelines will save time now and later:

1 *Don't waste time while you are doing your general reading.* Some students waste time by plodding along, reading every word of every sentence. Remember what your reading teacher told you years ago: you need to "shift gears" as you read, adjusting your speed to the content. For this preliminary reading, use high gear. Skim. Look for headings. Check the overall organization. Then read for topic sentences and summary paragraphs. If the text is not set off with headings and subheadings, try reading the first and last sentences of every paragraph. When something catches your eye, stop and read the entire segment.

2 *Note any bibliographies found in general reading.* Books and periodicals listed in bibliographies of general references will probably be on your "must read" list later. Keep a record of them. Likewise, note authors' names. Those that appear in general references will no doubt have published similar materials in other sources. They are authorities whose works may be valuable to you. Making note of these references now will save time later.

In addition, because this part of the research process must move quickly, follow this general time management plan:

Number of weeks to work on final paper	Number of days available to do preliminary reading and outline
10	4
8	3
6	2
4	1

TWO STUDENTS' PROGRESS

Sarah and Terry face very different responsibilities at this preliminary stage of research. Let's check in with them.

Sarah

My general topic was wetlands, but of course that was too broad. So I did some reading first in the online *Encyclopedia Americana*. When I looked up "Wetlands," the cross-reference said, "See Swamp, Marsh, Tidal Marsh." So under "Swamp" I found five headings:

Formation
Stages of Evolution into Dry Land
Plant and Animal Life
Characteristics
Importance

I skimmed the entire article because I really didn't know anything about wetlands. I just keep hearing about them. So I was mildly curious about their formation and had no idea that they sometimes naturally evolved into dry land. I had a rather warped idea about the plant and animal life because I always thought of swamps as filled with creepy, crawly things. The section on characteristics helped me understand what makes a marsh a marsh. But I was most interested in the section titled "Importance." In fact, I saw myself in that section when the writer said that some people think of swamps as "wastelands."

Then I decided to make a quick check of the library's other online encyclopedias. That's when I began pulling together ideas. When I typed in "wetlands," I found out that the term refers to lots of different areas: swamps, marshes, bogs, muskegs, moors, heaths, tidal marshes, mangrove forests, cypress swamps—on and on! Since I think best on paper, I decided to put my ideas into a concept web. This is what I scribbled out:

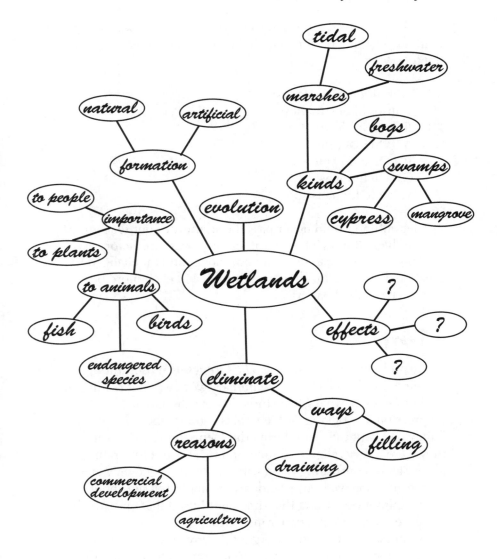

I began thinking about the importance of all these areas. If they are so important, what happens when we drain them or fill them to build a new shopping center or housing development? Could I do my paper on the effects of destroying wetlands? I worded my research question as follows: What are the effects of destroying wetlands? The purpose of my paper would be to identify the causes of that destruction and then determine the effects of that destruction.

With a narrowed topic and a clarified purpose, I was ready to write my working outline. Guided by my concept web, I wrote the following:

I. Definition of wetlands
II. Causes of destruction
III. Effects of destruction
    A. On plant life
    B. On animal life
    C. On humans
IV. Value to humans

That outline would never pass the scrutiny of our teacher if I were to hand it in as a final outline, but it was satisfactory as a working outline. I can tell you now, though, that it changed a great deal before I finished my research and even more before I finished my final paper!

Terry

My preliminary reading was *The Grapes of Wrath*, the assigned novel. In fact, my preliminary work was not reading at all, but recalling what I had studied about the Great Depression and talking with my folks. I remembered that my family had kept the farm during the Depression. I also knew they were a very religious family, and these ideas set up the potential for contrasting them with the Joads. My family and I were guessing what my grandparents might tell me about their experiences during that time, and I used that guesswork to figure out where my paper might go.

Of course, our topic was assigned, so my task was simply to choose a narrowed focus. I worded my research question this way: How did the characters in *The Grapes of Wrath* compare with my grandparents in their struggle through the Great Depression? My purpose was to compare the two families. So far I didn't have much to put in a working outline, but I came up with the following:

I. Grandfather's experiences
    A. Maintained family
    B. Earned living
    C. Farmed

    II. Joads' experiences
        A. Family broken
        B. Lost living
        C. Traveled

I wasn't really happy with this outline, but until I talked with my grandfather, I couldn't have anything more specific. Of course, the outline helped me plan my interview questions as well as my research. And after all, that's what our teacher says a working outline should do!

TIPS AND TRAPS

Sarah and Terry both offer the same advice at this stage of the research process. As Sarah explained, "It's easy to sit and stare at a blank page for hours without writing that working outline. I finally set a time limit for myself—20 minutes. Then I *made* myself get something down on paper within that time limit."

Terry continued, "If you start off behind schedule, you'll never catch up! I did the same thing Sarah did. I *made* myself quit staring at that blank page, moaning about not knowing what to write. Simply putting words on paper gets me going, even if I change it all later."

CHECKLIST FOR THE WORKING OUTLINE

You should be able to answer "yes" to the following questions about your preliminary work.

1. Have I narrowed my topic successfully?
2. Have I worded my topic as a question?
3. Have I clarified my purpose?
4. Does the outline include headings that will give me the chance to answer key questions about my topic?
5. Does the outline include headings that, when developed into a full research paper, will meet my purpose?
6. Does the outline reflect the key ideas addressed in my general reading?
7. Is the number of main headings appropriate for the assigned length of the paper?

EXERCISES

Exercise A: Evaluating Working Outlines

Directions: Evaluate working outlines illustrated in this chapter by thinking about and discussing the following questions.

1. Sarah's outline (page 32) is short. Is it too short for a satisfactory working outline for a 1,500–2,000-word paper? Why or why not?
2. Sarah's outline does not reflect all of the topics illustrated in her concept web (see page 31). Should those topics be included in her working outline? Why or why not?
3. Terry's outline (pages 32–33) has only two divisions. Is that adequate for a working outline for an 800–1,000-word paper? Why or why not?
4. Terry admits he is unhappy with his outline (page 33). Why do you think he is unhappy?
5. Terry has confined his preliminary reading to the assigned novel. In light of his assignment, do you think he needs to do other preliminary reading to improve his working outline? Why or why not?
6. Apply logic to Sarah's outline. What illogical divisions do you see? Why?
7. Apply logic to Terry's outline. What illogical divisions do you see? Why?
8. Study the outline for laser technology (page 28). The outline lacks balance since section III has numerous subdivisions but section II has none. Is that a problem for a working outline? Why or why not?
9. What general statements can you make about working outlines as illustrated in these three models?
10. How do you think a final outline will differ from these working outlines?

Exercise B: Creating a Working Outline

Directions: Use the questions that follow to generate a satisfactory working outline for Beth's paper. Her topic: How do Japanese working conditions compare with those in the United States? Her paper's purpose: to analyze why Japanese workers, as contrasted to American workers, often stay with the same company until they retire.

1. Do Japan's employers pay comparable wages to U.S. employers?
2. What health benefits are available for each?

3. Why do some Japanese workers think taking a job is like joining a family?
4. Do Japanese workers never change jobs?
5. Do they ever change companies?
6. What job security does each group of workers have? How has this changed in Japan in the last decade?
7. Does Japan have labor unions?
8. Do Japanese workers contribute to management decisions?
9. Do they have retirement benefits?
10. Is quality control necessary in Japan?
11. Are Japanese workers ever fired?
12. What keeps each group of workers productive?

Exercise C: Creating Your Own Working Outline

Directions: Create a list of questions (see page 27 for a model) or draw a concept web (see page 31 for a model) for your own topic. Then use those ideas to generate your own working outline.

3

Locating the Secondary Print Resources

Primary resources are the materials that are contemporary to your subject—a book, an interview, a survey response, a letter. Secondary resources, on the other hand, are secondhand materials written later about someone or something. Compare these examples: If you are writing a paper about John James Audubon, then his diaries, paintings, and books are primary sources. However, books, magazine articles, and essays about Audubon, his life, and his work are secondary resources. If you are writing a paper about Emily Dickinson, her poetry and personal letters are primary sources; but her biography and books and articles about her and her poetry are secondary resources. Take the idea a step farther: if you conduct interviews, surveys, and experiments and write up the results, your written work then becomes a secondary resource for someone else! Depending on your purpose and your topic, secondary references may be sufficient. This book examines your use of secondary print resources in this chapter and Web resources in the following chapter.

With your working outline as your guide, you are ready to search the library. Your search will take you to several parts of the library: the general reference section's online or other catalogs for both books and periodicals, and, of course, into the library stacks to find specific references. You will also find yourself using the World Wide Web, where reliability of sources becomes a major issue in the research process. This chapter and the next are designed to guide you through that multifaceted search.

TRADITIONAL SOURCES AND THE WEB

They say you can find anything on the Web, so why worry about books and periodicals? With more than 150 million Web sites out there, surely everything you need to know is only a few clicks away. That's a common misconception about research, especially among student researchers. (More on Web research in the next chapter.)

Good research requires a balance of print and online sources for a very simple reason: You really cannot find everything on the Web. Many of the most credible resources are found only in print, not on the Web. And of course the broader your range of resources, the better your research report will be. So even if you do find everything you need on the Web to complete your KWL chart, your search is inadequate. Good research means that you search multiple kinds of resources, including hard copy.

But let's clarify what we mean by "print." Print materials (books, general references, magazines, newspapers, leaflets, and other documents) are frequently available online, often in complete text with photos, maps, charts, whatever—just as originally published in hard copy. So "online" is not the same as "Web" resources.

For the moment, here's what you should do:

- If your topic IS NOT recent, explore your school or local library's **catalog** for books on the subject. For instance, if you're doing research on the sphinx, check the online catalog for subjects like Egyptian architecture or sphinx. Then take a look at those books for clues about your search.
- If your subject IS recent, check whatever periodical index (usually online or CD-ROM) your library carries. For instance, if you're doing research on the current election campaign, check the index for subjects like election campaigns, political campaigns, or candidates' names.

GENERAL REFERENCES

Libraries have a separate section called "Reference." Get to know this section of your library, for it is filled with valuable information for research papers. Check with your school librarian or media specialist for recommendations on print or online versions of the following kinds of resources.

> **dictionaries**—abridged and unabridged, for English and foreign languages, both general and subject-specific, including references like *The International Dictionary of Thoughts,*

Dictionary of Problem Words and Expressions, McGraw-Hill Dictionary of Scientific and Technical Terms, Dictionary of American Slang, World Dictionary of Foreign Expressions, and *Dictionary of Classical Mythology*

thesauri—references that show synonyms and antonyms, like *Webster's New Explorer Thesaurus, Roget's International Thesaurus,* and *American Heritage Thesaurus for Learners of English*

encyclopedias—both general, like the *Encyclopedia Americana,* and the specific, like the *Encyclopedia of Social Sciences, Encyclopedia of World Literature in the 20th Century, Encyclopedia of Careers and Vocational Guidance, Encyclopedia of Women in the Ancient World, Social Issues in Science and Technology: An Encyclopedia, Encyclopedia of Archaeology,* and *Oxford Encyclopedia of Theatre and Performance*

indexes—references that show where information can be found, like *Play Index, Short Story Index, Granger's Index to Poetry,* and online databases with their own indexes, like *EBSCOhost, Infotrac, Expanded Academic ASAP, NewsBank Info Web,* and *SIRS* (see the special section on indexes below)

yearbooks—annual chronicles of a single year, like *Facts on File, Statesman's Yearbook, Britannica Book of the Year,* and *Book of the States*

almanacs—storehouses of miscellaneous facts and statistics, published annually, like the *World Almanac and Book of Facts, Statistical Abstract of the United Slates, Sports Illustrated Sports Almanac,* and *Chase's Calendar of Events*

biographical dictionaries—collections of sketches of lives of individuals, like *Current Biography, Who's Who in America, Great Lives from History, American National Biography,* and *Contemporary Musicians*

directories—references listing names and addresses of people, organizations, and institutions, like *Complete Directory for People with Disabilities, America's Best Colleges, Foundation Grants Directory,* and *Encyclopedia of Associations*

atlases—books of maps and charts, like the *American Heritage Pictorial Atlas of United States History, Goode's World Atlas, Atlas of Cyberspace, Atlas of the World's Deserts,* and *Penguin Atlas of Food*

gazetteers—collections of geographical information and data about places, like the *World Atlas and Gazetteer* or *Columbia Gazetteer of the World*

periodical publications—newspapers, newsletters, and journals, like *The New York Times, Newsweek,* and *U.S. News & World Report* (most or all of which are probably online in full text through your library's subscription services)

TECH TIP

Many general references appear in electronic form. On-line and CD-ROM resources include entire sets of encyclopedias, collections of history books, dictionaries, and other reference books. You can make quick subject searches of these electronic forms because they allow multiple ways to search with just a few keystrokes. Likewise, some general reference works can be accessed on the Web. Simply enter the reference title as a keyword search in a search engine like Google.

LIBRARY CATALOG SYSTEMS

All books in the library are arranged according to one of two classification systems: the Dewey decimal system or the Library of Congress system. Both systems move from the general to the particular, but one uses numbers and the other uses letters and numbers.

The Dewey decimal system uses numbers 000–900 for its main divisions. The Library of Congress system, on the other hand, uses the 26 letters of the alphabet for main divisions. Although most high schools use the Dewey decimal cataloging system, most universities and many public libraries use the Library of Congress system. Thus, you must learn to use both systems.

Dewey Decimal System

The Dewey decimal system is arranged in ten main classes as follows:

000—Generalities
100—Philosophy
200—Religion
300—Social Sciences
400—Languages

500—Pure Science
600—Technology
700—Art and Recreation
800—Literature
900—History

The main classes are subdivided by number and subdivided again with decimals, author reference, and title reference. Compare these three books:

Call Number	Title	Author
930 C82a	*Ancient History*	Arnold Collins
930 C82o	*An Outline of Ancient History*	Arnold Collins
936.7 C82e	*Early European History*	Arnold Collins

In order to find books shelved by the Dewey decimal system, read from left to right and top to bottom. For instance, the following series of numbers represents the way books would be arranged on the shelf:

227	227	227.032	227.1	227.1355	227.14
An2b	J52a	C32c	Am4s	K24p	C12n

A call number is not unique, and ten books in the system could all have the same call number, for example, 220 B. So, be sure to check the second and third lines (called "Cutter numbers") as well as titles!

Library of Congress System

Most universities use the Library of Congress system to catalog books. The system uses the 26 letters of the alphabet (except I, O, W, X, and Y, letters reserved for further expansion) to create main divisions:

A— General Works
B— Philosophy, Psychology, Religion
C— Auxiliary Sciences of History
D— History: General and Old World (Eastern Hemisphere)
E–F— History: American (Western Hemisphere)
G— Geography, Maps, Anthropology, Recreation
H— Social Sciences
J— Political Science
K— Law
L— Education

M—Music
N—Fine Arts
P—Philology, Linguistics, Languages, Literature
Q—Science
R—Medicine
S—Agriculture
T—Technology
U—Military Science
V—Naval Science
Z—Bibliography, Library Science

These main divisions are subdivided by adding a second letter. Numbers add further divisions.

In order to find shelved books using the Library of Congress system, use the same procedures as you do for the Dewey decimal system, reading left to right and top to bottom. For instance, these books will be arranged on the shelf as follows:

PN	PN	PN	PN	PN	PN	PN	PN
2	87	87	1995.8	1996	7123	7123	7891
B56	L34	L5	K6523	D1	M62	M9	.C8
							B38

CATALOG SEARCHES

Regardless of the cataloging system a library uses, it will have an index to almost every book in the facility. The original means of indexing books was the card catalog. For each book, there were three kinds of cards in the card catalog: author card, title card, and subject card. The author card was the primary card. The title card and subject cards were identical to the author card with the addition of the title or subject heading above the author's name. Efficient researchers used the card catalog to tell them whether or not a book was worth their attention.

Most libraries no longer use a card catalog but have replaced it with a computer catalog, a much faster, easier, and generally more fruitful index than the traditional card catalog. Now we refer to a book's "record" rather than its card catalog cards, and the record is filled with information to aid your search. Even though each computer system works slightly differently, all follow a general pattern. Thus, we can make generic statements about how to use the systems.

Like card catalogs, computer catalogs have title, author, and subject searches. Unlike card catalogs, most computer catalogs also have keyword searches; and also unlike card catalogs, computer catalogs include a resource's availability—available, checked out, on reserve, and so on. Most systems are quite user-friendly and have on-screen directions or help screens accessible from the opening screen. Since the computer catalog at your public library will most likely be different from your school's computer catalog, you will need to read the on-screen directions for each and follow them carefully.

If you used the computer catalog the same way researchers once used the card catalog, you would turn first to subject screens. Keep in mind, however, that the subject screens reflect broad subjects, not necessarily the narrowed topic you have chosen for your research paper. If you find nothing in a computer subject search under a heading that matches your topic, look for a broader topic. For instance, if you do not find "wetlands," then look for "ecology" or "environment." When you find a book on the broad topic, check the table of contents and index for your narrowed topic. When you find a particularly good book, check the "subject" headings on the record. By clicking on one of those subjects, your catalog search will take you directly to other books on the same subject. Since subject headings (as opposed to keywords) are standardized vocabulary, they function almost like categories. Take advantage of this helpful search device to find additional material.

CRITICAL THINKING HINT

1. Consider the following: If you find an entire book on your topic, your topic is too broad! It follows logically that you probably will not find your "narrowed" topic as a subject heading in an online catalog search.
2. Just because you find nothing in an initial search does not mean that your library has nothing on your topic. Keep trying different keywords. Think of synonyms. Check a thesaurus.
3. When you find one book that is especially promising, try an author search for other books by that author. Chances are he or she has written other materials on the same general subject—both books and magazine articles.

4. If the computer catalog sends you to a book that includes a bibliography, be sure to look for those references. Your library may have those books or periodical articles as well, but perhaps your search did not locate these materials because they were cataloged under a different heading.

Let's follow Muriel as she begins her search for books that include information about General Sherman's occupation of Savannah in 1864. Where should she start? With "Savannah"? She probably will not find much there, but if she finds a book on the history of Savannah, she may find a few pages or paragraphs. What next? "Sherman"? Maybe. At least she may find a biography. Then what? "Civil War"? Oops. Wrong heading. See "United States—History," the cross-reference says.

Finding sources is, indeed, a detective game. For a paper on theater architecture in Elizabethan England, Jana entered "Globe Theater" and found nothing. So where should she look next? She tried a broader topic: "Shakespeare." Tonya is working on a paper about the effect of pesticides on apples and looked up "apples"; she found nothing. What next? She tried a broader topic: "fruit." Kevin is writing about the migratory patterns of salmon. There was nothing under the topic "salmon." His next try was with broader topics: "fish" and "fishing."

When you find listings for books that sound promising, jot down title, author, and call number. Since many libraries shelve older books in the closed stacks (shelves not open to the public), you may have to fill out a form, referred to as a "call slip," to request books from there. Whether you fill out a form for the librarian or only make notes for yourself, double-check the call number. Without an accurate number, no one can find the book.

CATALOG KEYWORD SEARCHES

Since the typical title, author, and subject searches are much the same in both print and computer catalogs, we will turn our attention now to a feature unique to computer records: the keyword search. If your general reading turned up an important—or key—word, you may find good references by searching for that word. Although the keyword search is similar to a subject search, it will find keywords in titles, subject headings, notes, tables of contents—searching the entire record. Such a search may address a much broader subject, books otherwise not listed in a subject search.

For example, Beth looked up "Japanese business" but found nothing in the subject search. She did a search under "Japan and business" and found several books. Those, in turn, led her to others. Likewise, Connie searched for the subject "Pictographs" and found nothing; but when she ran a keyword search with the same term, she not only found a book but also cross-references to "Delaware Indians—Language." These led her to others.

You cannot be sloppy about searching topics in the computer catalog. For example, if you use the keyword "aids," you will get listings about teaching aids, former President Reagan's hearing aid, legal aids, a book titled *Indiana: The Early Years* (because it includes a chapter "Finding Aids"), a book on pathology (because it includes color aids in dentistry), and a business book (because it includes management services practice aids), as well as Acquired Immune Deficiency Syndrome. Reading a good general article about your topic first will help you choose accurate, precise search words.

CRITICAL THINKING HINT

The most efficient use of computer catalogs results when you understand Boolean logic, the basis for modern computer systems. A way to look at Boolean logic is through these diagrams.

 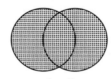 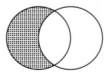

A *and* B   A *or* B   A *not* B

The Boolean search strategy ties words together to more precisely define your needs and thereby direct the computer's search. If you ask for a subject word of "dog" with no Boolean operator, you will get listings about dogs, dog pounds, dog shows, dog food, etc. But if you use a Boolean operator and link "dog" with a second subject of "shows," you will get listings only about dog shows. (See page 64 for more details about Boolean operators.)

Consider Roland's experience. He is writing a research paper about Shakespeare's play *Hamlet*. Consider the options for his search:

1. When he typed in "Shakespeare" as author, he got a listing of all of Shakespeare's works found in the library—156 entries.
2. When he typed in "Shakespeare" as title, he was overwhelmed by listings of books about Shakespeare—biographies and critical essays—234 entries.
3. When he typed in "Shakespeare" as subject, he was overwhelmed by listings both by and about the playwright/poet—187 headings.
4. When he typed in "Shakespeare" for a keyword search, he was REALLY overwhelmed by listings both by and about the playwright/poet as well as listings about Shakespeare fishing equipment and John Shakespeare—764 listings.
5. When he typed in "Hamlet" as title, he found only copies of the play, critical works that include "Hamlet" as part of their titles, plus a few other non-Shakespearean works that include "Hamlet" as part of their titles—19 entries.
6. When he typed in "Hamlet" as subject, he found only two listings—including one referring to the motion picture.
7. When he typed in "Hamlet" for a keyword search, he found essays about the Shakespearean play as well as a book, *The Hamlet*, by William Faulkner—61 entries.

On the other hand, when Roland *refined* his search request, he quickly found the references he needed for his paper, material about Shakespeare's *Hamlet*. How? He used a Boolean operator with his keyword search. That gave the computer a specific search path rather than the general subject, author, or title searches that call up every entry in the broad topic. The following illustrates:

type	*shakespeare and hamlet*	= 50 listings
type	*hamlet and critic$*	= 20 listings
	(see page 46 for explanation of $)	

Then the listings are confined to those *about* Shakespeare's *Hamlet*. The search is fast and easy!

TECH TIP

Most online catalog systems offer drop-down menus to select author, title, or keyword searches. Most will also offer the opportunity to use truncation.

Truncation (the use of a symbol like $) lets you retrieve variant forms. If you type in "tropic$" you will retrieve "tropics," "tropical," and so on. Different systems use different truncation symbols. Check with your librarian.

WARNING: In order to be successful in any computer search, you must follow two guidelines:

1. You must spell correctly. If you ask for Moore when you should have asked for More, you will not get what you need.
2. You must be impeccably logical. That means you must be able to think of precise synonyms and accurate descriptors as well as establish clear relationships.

PERIODICAL INDEXES

In order to find just the right periodicals for your research, whether you're looking for magazines or newspapers, indexes—both electronic and print—show the way. While many databases provide these indexes, your library may or may not subscribe to them. So your first task is to find out which indexes are available to you and what they index.

Some databases index as many as 3,000 periodicals, many in full text on screen. Like computer catalogs, the electronic magazine and newspaper indexes offer multiple search avenues. On some systems, you can limit a keyword search by combining it with a range of dates, magazines, newspapers, or a paired keyword. Unlike computer catalogs, many periodical indexes provide search results for magazines that include a one-paragraph summary—or abstract—of the article.

Since electronic indexes differ dramatically from one another, learn to check directions carefully and access "Help" screens for best results.

Some systems will allow you to print a copy of the entire results list, a list of only those references in the library, or a list of only selected abstracts. And most also allow users to e-mail full-text articles or custom lists to themselves.

Second, the Web carries hundreds of magazines in electronic form—or e-zines, as they are called. You can find current issues as well as back issues. Most provide access by topic or by magazine. New Web pages spring up daily, so look for other sites as well.

OTHER MEDIA

In addition to books and periodicals, you may find valuable resources in other media. Consider the vertical file, microforms, and audiovisuals.

Vertical File

The vertical file (sometimes called the pamphlet file) includes pamphlets, clippings, and government publications. It takes only minutes to check, so the time can be well spent. For instance, Sarah found quite a stack of current pamphlets about wetlands, some with bibliographies and others with government e-mail addresses. Some libraries enter the subject headings for the pamphlet file in the online catalog. Ask at your library.

Microforms

Microforms, any microphotographically produced material, will be beneficial to almost everyone. The microforms include microfilm, microprint, microcards, and microfiche. Many publications were put in microform simply because thousands of volumes can be stored in a space about the size of a shoe box. Still, shoe boxes add up, and the special equipment needed to read the microforms (which also takes space) is expensive to buy and maintain. Thus, crowded libraries have switched to electronic forms, and microforms are slowly disappearing. Nevertheless, if your library has microforms, you will no doubt find them a valuable resource. Online catalogs usually indicate what titles for which years are microforms.

Audiovisuals

Depending on your topic, you might find helpful resources among the media center's collection of audio and/or videotapes, CD music recordings, DVDs, prints, mounted pictures, posters, and transparencies. Be sure to ask.

OTHER SEARCH IDEAS

Beyond the usual catalogs and indexes, four other possible sources often yield good materials.

Interlibrary Loans

When an important source is not available in a local library, it is possible that you can get that book through an interlibrary loan. That is, your public or university library may have the service that allows it to borrow the book from another library and in turn lend it to you. There are several drawbacks. First, the book is not readily available, so if you are rushed for time, forget it. It can sometimes take two weeks or more to get a book on interlibrary loan. Second, even if your library finds the book you need elsewhere, it may be checked out from that library. Third, the service is not free. You may be expected to pay the postage for shipping the book from and back to the lending library; there may be an insurance charge; some libraries collect a service fee; and there may be a copying charge for reference materials. Unless your paper depends on this resource, you may be better off seeking alternative sources.

Federal, State, and Local Government

Some branch of the federal government will most likely have information about your topic. The *United States Government Organizational Manual* will help you decide which departments, agencies, or bureaus deal with your topic. *U.S. Government on the Web* and *Government Information on the Internet* are two additional books updated regularly that help you find those departments, agencies, or bureaus on the Web. Your congressional representative can also help. Call his or her local office or write to the Washington, D.C. office with a *specific* request (NOT "send me what you have"). Many government printing office publications and documents are available free for the asking. If you write, allow four to six weeks for delivery.

Local and state offices, while more limited in their resources, usually respond more quickly, especially if you can make a personal visit to the office involved.

TECH TIP

To reach your congressional representative quickly, e-mail him or her. Newer reference books include e-mail addresses for those legislators who are willing to post them.

To telephone your representative on a toll-free 800 or 888 number, check the toll-free number directory on the Web. You can find it at several sites. Do a keyword search by asking for "800 directory." Or reach him or her by e-mail through <www.house.gov> or <www.senate.gov>. Each site is searchable by zip code or city and state.

Associations

Almost any topic will have some kind of association supporting its cause, whether it is the potato growers' association, the chocolate candy producers' association, or whatever. These people are experts in their fields and often have publications free for the asking and information-rich Web sites. To find the appropriate association, check the index, *Encyclopedia of Associations* (published by Gale Research), available in most public and university libraries. You can also write to the American Society of Association Executives, ASAE Building, 1575 I St. N.W., Washington, D.C. 20005, or phone them at 888–950–2723. Check them on the Web at <http://www.asaenet.org>. Associations can provide up-to-date statistics and news as well as general information.

Museums

Depending on your topic, a museum may be able to offer help. Many museums maintain libraries and may allow you to use those materials on the premises. Their resource people, always experts in their fields, can offer advice as well. (These people may also serve as excellent primary sources. Keep them in mind for Chapter 6.)

You can also write to special museums with *specific* questions (NOT "send me what you have"). Your local library will have an index of special museums. If you have a specific question relating to the general areas of art, history, air and space, zoology, horticulture, and marine life, you may write the Smithsonian Institution Inquiry Mail Service, Washington, D.C. 20560. Allow six weeks for an answer to your query.

TECH TIP

You can tap the resources of many civil and government associations as well as many United States and world museums on the Internet. Consider whether these sites may help you with your topic (and find others using various search engines).

NASA <http://www.nasa.gov>
Bureau of Labor Statistics <http://stats.bls.gov>
U.S. Census <http://www.census.gov>
Census Bureau data maps <http://www.census.gov/geo/www/maps>
First Gov: the U.S. government's official Web portal <http://firstgov.gov>
FedWorld Information Network <http://www.fedworld.gov>
State and local governments <http://lcweb.loc.gov/global/state/stategov.html>
U.S. House of Representatives home page <http://www.house.gov>
United States Senate <http://www.senate.gov>
Better Business Bureau <http://www.cbbb.org/>
CIA publications <http://www.odci.gov/cia/sitemap.html>
Library of Congress <http://lcweb.loc.gov>

TIME MANAGEMENT GUIDELINES

Finding time to go to the library is never easy for busy students. In order to do a good search and work effectively with materials that cannot be removed from the library, plan to spend several hours in the library. You will be most efficient if you plan a single block of time for intensive work. If that is not possible and you must break up the time into smaller segments, you will be less efficient, so allow extra total time. Chances are, you will also need to go back later to make a quick check of one thing or another.

Whether or not you use the Internet, you will necessarily do a careful search of the library. Nevertheless, in spite of the amount of time you will need to spend at the library, this part of the research process will go rather quickly. The time may seem greater simply because it must be spent in a specific place—not at home where you can stop for phone calls or for your favorite television show. Use the following general guidelines to manage your time effectively:

Number of weeks to work on final paper	Number of days available to find secondary print resources
10	4
8	3
6	2
4	1

TWO STUDENTS' PROGRESS

As you can probably guess, Sarah and Terry faced different problems when they began researching their topics. Listen to their experiences as they share hints and surprises.

Sarah

As you know, I began my search with general encyclopedia articles. After that, since my topic was current, I knew I wanted to rely on periodicals. Fortunately, our library has a computer magazine search that provides abstracts of the articles and tells me which magazines are carried in the library. So I asked for a broad heading—wetlands. That turned up over 100 listings. When I checked to see how many of those listings were in our library, the list shortened to about 70. So I began skimming the abstracts on screen. I found some funny things. One article, for instance, was about a café in New York. Since it is called Wetlands, it showed up in my search. That suggested that I needed to use a more precise descriptor!

Since I was interested only in the environmental impact of the destruction of wetlands, I decided to try two limiting words: *environ$* (so I would get *environment*) and *destruction*. That pair of words turned out to be too limiting (only two articles), so I dropped *destruction*. That gave me a respectable list of about 30 references—still too many to check out and haul home. So next I skimmed the specific references. Several entries were a page or less, so I scrapped them. Several other entries were from the same issue of the same magazine, and that turned out to be a special issue just on the general topic of wetlands. Good source. Next I noticed that a number of the articles were in farm magazines. I put question marks beside those. I didn't know whether I'd need them or not. Maybe later.

For good measure, I checked the computer catalog and tried several kinds of searches. Here's what happened. The subject search was too broad, but keyword searches with different Boolean operators finally led me to nine good listings. Five were more than ten years old, so I hunted up the remaining four books on the shelves and checked the tables of contents and the indexes for topics on my working outline. Three had enough material to make it worth my while to check them out.

My total time in the library—including searching indexes and catalogs for magazines, newspapers, and books; finding books and magazines; deciding which were appropriate and checking them out—was about four hours.

Terry

Actually, I had the option of doing very little searching. Since our main reference was supposed to be the novel itself, we had to seek only general information about the Great Depression and critical commentary about the novel. Because all of us would need the same resources, our teacher put on reserve in the school library the books pertinent to our topic. That meant we didn't have to do the search. It also meant, however, that we all had to find time to work in the library when no one else was using the sources.

My school day is packed with extra lab duties and volunteer work in the office. My best work time is after dinner in the evening, so I chose to go to the public library. That gave me two advantages: I found resources that other students didn't use, and I could check out these resources and read and work at home. I found a few surprises in my search.

When I looked up "Depression" in the computer catalog, I found all kinds of references to mental depression and virtually nothing about the Great Depression. When I asked for "Great Depression," I found nothing. Then I asked for "US History" and found 17 listings. I knew that couldn't be right, so I asked for "America$ and history." That brought up 5,421— yes, count 'em—listings. It was rather obvious I needed to limit that search! Then I tried "depression and history" and found 25 entries. Of these 25, I identified one really on-target title. Then I looked at the Library of Congress subject heading on the record. The heading was "Depressions—1929—United States." That was a hyperlink, and it led me to more highly relevant books. I used the call numbers from those entries to find the general area in the library and then thumbed through the most promising books.

At the same time, I did a keyword search about the author, John Steinbeck (56 entries), and added a Boolean operator to narrow the search to "Steinbeck and grapes" and found seven entries—the specific sources I needed!

My total time in the library was about two hours.

TIPS AND TRAPS

When you begin looking for books on your topic, keep in mind what your working outline calls for. As Sarah explained, "I could find lots of books about environmental issues, but I needed information only on wetlands. Then I found entire books about wetlands, so I used my working outline as a guide by which to narrow the search and to check the tables of contents and the indexes to see if books included information I could use." Both Terry and Sarah said they wouldn't bother with books that didn't include an index. "You'll just never find what you need if there isn't an index," Terry explained.

Another experience caused Terry to comment, "When I went to the library to find material about the Great Depression, I didn't want whole books about the era. I really needed concise information, like a single chapter in a larger reference. So I found the area in which those books were shelved, and then began thumbing through the tables of contents and indexes. No one expected us to read entire volumes about the Great Depression!"

Try learning from Terry's experience. When you find several suitable references cataloged, look them up on the shelves. Then look around at other books nearby. You may find something useful.

Finally, a tip about relationships with librarians. The following observations come from librarians themselves who say repeatedly that students generally aren't aware of the best ways to partner with librarians for research help. Do you find yourself in any of these categories? If so, change your habits and improve your rapport with your friendly librarian.

1. Some students never ask for help, flounder around ineffectively on their own, and become very frustrated. Librarians can and want to help. It's their job!

2. Others approach librarians for help but seem unable to articulate what it is they need. Librarians cannot read your mind or think for you. Ask clear questions about specific problems. Make specific requests.

3. Worse yet, some students expect the librarian to "do it all." They seem to take the do-it-for-me attitude instead of the show-me-how-to-do-it attitude. The search is your job. When you are stumped, then ask the librarian to show you how.

4. A few students have been known to call the library asking for "everything you have" on a given subject and say they will pick up the materials in an hour. A librarian who puts up with that is very rare, so don't expect to get a positive response to such a rude request.

As one librarian put it, "Given the constraints of staffing and work flow, librarians want to be helpful and want to teach people about using the library. We can often give guidance and time-saving clarification to the search. We do need, however, the cooperation of students to do these things."

CHECKLIST FOR LOCATING SECONDARY RESOURCES

You should be able to answer "yes" to the following questions about your search for secondary resources.

1. Have I checked the logical general references for my topic: dictionaries, general and specific encyclopedias, indexes, almanacs,

biographical dictionaries, bibliographies (either in print or electronically)?

2. If my topic is not current, have I checked the computer catalog for books on my topic?
   a. In order to find more information, have I looked up headings broader than my narrowed topic?
   b. Have I looked for other books by authors of sources already discovered?
   c. Have I used keyword searches?
3. If my topic is rather current, have I checked a periodical index?
   a. In order to find more information, have I looked up headings broader than my narrowed topic?
   b. Have I used keyword searches?
4. Have I looked for materials listed in bibliographies included in books or articles I've already discovered?
5. Have I consulted other appropriate indexes?
   a. If my topic is specialized, have I checked the specialized indexes, like *Education Index* (or online *Education Abstracts*), *Book Review Digest*, or *General Science Abstracts*?
   b. Have I checked newspaper indexes like *Newsbank* or *Newspaper Source*?
6. Have I considered nonbook media, like pamphlets, government publications, clippings, microforms, films, or other audiovisual references?
7. Have I considered other sources, like government agencies, associations, and museums?

EXERCISES

Exercise A: *Finding Sources*

Directions: Name a source in which you could find the following information.

1. Lee Iacocca's immigrant origins
2. NFL individual lifetime, season, and game records
3. Map of U.S. territories between 1820 and 1854
4. List of children's poems about foxes
5. Why Noboru Takeshita is known in Japan as "a behind-the-scenes consensus builder"
6. A critical evaluation of the poems, books, and recordings by May Swenson

7. Author John Steinbeck's obituary (died in 1968)
8. Who said, "Men are born equal but they are also born different"
9. When to use *interior* or *internal* and when to use *continual* or *continuous*
10. What the French mean when they refer to a *feuilleton télévise*
11. The population of Panama
12. A review of James Michener's *Legacy,* published in 1988
13. A list of articles about the effectiveness of letters to parents to keep them informed about their children's progress in school
14. Six words that rhyme with "fifty"
15. Weekly digest of world news
16. General properties of radio waves

Exercise B: Naming Other Headings

Part 1

Directions: Check a periodical index to find out under which other headings you will find information on the following topics.

1. Radioactive pollution
2. Landscape gardening
3. Japanese electronics industries
4. Migration

Part 2

Directions: Check a periodical index to determine which subheadings the following topics include.

1. Baltimore
2. Venus
3. Smoking
4. Birds

Exercise C: Choosing Appropriate Keywords

Directions: Assume that the following are topics for which students need to do research. Name the index or catalog in which they should look, and recommend at least four keywords under which they should search for sources.

1. film version (as contrasted to the stage version) of *Hamlet*
2. effects of the Dred Scott decision
3. aftermath of the Chernobyl nuclear catastrophe
4. effects of cable television on NBC, ABC, and CBS
5. impact of computer crimes on ordinary citizens

6. discoveries of *Voyager II*
7. Frank Lloyd Wright's influence on furniture design
8. Robert Frost's poetic imagery
9. ways to encourage recycling at home and at work
10. common characteristics of Broadway's five longest-running plays (This one is tricky. You'll need two sources.)

Searching the Web

Once you've searched library resources, both in print and online, you are ready to check the World Wide Web resources. Searching the Web, however, is more than just clicking randomly on interesting links. Rather, you have a specific goal: to follow your working outline and to complete your KWL chart.

Your first step in doing serious Web research is to consider the search engines or directories you'll be using.

SEARCH ENGINES AND DIRECTORIES

Your computer has a Web browser as part of its software, probably either Netscape or Internet Explorer. In either case, the Web browser is like a telephone. It can dial up any of hundreds of thousands of Web sites. These sites are like the numbers listed in the telephone directory. But it's such a massive telephone directory that we need something like a directory assistance operator. In computer language, that's called a search engine.

A search engine lets you enter a keyword or phrase that reflects what you want to learn. When you click the *Search button*, the search engine looks through the Web for matches to your word or phrase. The problem is that not all search engines are the same. Here's why:

- Not every search engine searches the same files.
- Not every search engine searches the same number of files.

- Not all search engines access newspapers or magazines.
- No one search engine searches the entire Web.

Directories can also help you find information, but they work very differently from search engines. In fact, they serve an altogether different purpose.

Directories are organized by human beings who are experts in their respective fields. Thus, directories give you very different information than do search engines. The advantage of directories, of course, is that they have the human touch, so to speak.

Some sites are only search engines, like Google (http://www. google.com). Some search engines include directories, like Yahoo! (http:// www.yahoo.com).

Sometimes directories are called **subject catalogs**. Don't let the terminology confuse you.

So you need to know when—or whether—to search a directory or use a search engine. Here are the basic differences.

Directories	Search Engines
- Work like the Yellow Pages of your phone book, when you look up a business or service but don't know the business name	- Work like the White Pages of your phone book, when you look up the specific business name
- Serve best when you're browsing	- Serve best when you're searching
- Take you to the home page of a Web site and let you explore on your own	- Take you to a specific page where it finds matches to your search words or phrases
- Help you when you don't know exactly what you're looking for	- Help you when you know exactly what information you need
- Find the "big things," like a newspaper site or a music site or a line of lyrics	- Find the "detailed things," like a quotation from a newspaper column
- Are organized by human beings, experts in their respective fields	- Are organized mechanically, without thought processes; robotlike

Search engines and directories, however, are becoming more and more alike, especially as many search engines now incorporate directories.

So let's look more carefully at search engines. Using one search engine instead of another won't defeat your efforts at research. On the other hand, you never want to limit your search to one. In fact, you should use at least three different search engines for best results. The point is that the differences among search engines aren't radical, but there's no question that some search engines are easier to use than others. Some are better for certain topics than others, and some offer better search tools.

The following ten search engines, listed in alphabetical order, are a few among the 75 or so search engines worth your investigation:

> All the Web at <www.alltheweb.com>
> Alta Vista at <www.altavista.com>
> Ask Jeeves at <www.ask.com>
> Excite at <www.excite.com>
> Hotbot at <www.hotbot.com>
> Lycos at <www.lycos.com>
> Google at <www.google.com>
> Teoma at <www.teoma.com>
> Webcrawler at <www.webcrawler.com>
> Yahoo! at <www.yahoo.com>

TECH TIP

Depending on your topic, whether or not a search engine will search news headlines may not be an issue. But maybe you're researching a controversial topic. In that case, access to a discussion group on the topic may help you find the experts with the best arguments from their respective points of view. You'll want a search engine that helps you find that discussion group.

CRITICAL THINKING HINT

Some students develop a "brand" loyalty to a certain search engine or two. Don't be one of them! If you're shopping for new shoes, wouldn't you try on several pairs to see which feel the best? And then wouldn't you also check to see what store has the best price for that pair of shoes? Comparison shopping is smart, whether you're buying shoes or searching for information on the Web.

Even if you go back to the first store to buy the first pair of shoes you tried on, comparison shopping is the only way to know you've found the best deal.

There are also **meta-search engines**, or simply **meta-engines**. The difference is how much of the Web they search. As you might guess, a meta-search engine does a whopper search. It puts your keyword search through multiple other search engines and directories. Then some—but not all—of them combine all the results, weed out the repetitions, and rank the returns by relevancy.

CRITICAL THINKING HINT

While the meta-engine sounds like a dream come true, keep in mind that since it searches many other search engines, it can use only those operators used by ALL search engines. As a result, you lose some of the effective search features discussed later.

While new search engines, including meta-search engines, show up fairly regularly, you may want to check out two fairly popular ones (at least as of this writing):

> Dogpile at <http://www.dogpile.com>
> Metacrawler at <http://www.metacrawler.com>

THE GOOD SEARCH

Let's consider four basic principles of doing a good search.

First Principle: Use a Minimum of Three Search Engines

No matter which search engine you use first, you'll need to try the same or similar search with at least two others. Since not all search engines search the same parts of the Web, you'll want to explore the best you can. Just think: comparison shopping!

Second Principle: Consider the Relevancy of Results

Most search engines report by something called **relevance ranking**, meaning that the best matches, or *hits*, appear first. Let's say you enter a search word and get 60,842 matches. Before you moan and groan, remember that with relevance ranking, the first several dozen are probably the best matches. Of course, "best matches" is from the search engine's programming point of view, not from a human being's thought processes. So the search engine's best may not be the best for you. They may not all apply to your focused topic.

CRITICAL THINKING HINT

Even when you get the results ranked by relevance, don't waste time clicking on every site that shows up in your results list. Think first. Then pick the ones that make sense and are directly related to your focused topic.

Third Principle: Narrow the Search

When you get way too many hits, you'll need to refine your search term. Here are some ways to do that.

1. Choose a more accurate term. Instead of asking for "wetlands," ask for "estuary."
2. Add a limiting term. Instead of asking for "estuary," ask for "Chesapeake estuary."
3. Add multiple terms. Instead of asking for "wetlands," ask for "sewage treatment wetlands."

CRITICAL THINKING HINT

To help you think through the three items above, check your cluster map. And remember to refer regularly to your KWL chart in order to keep your search focused.

4. Start with your most important word. Instead of asking for "cat pet," ask for "pet cat" or, more specifically, "pet house cat."

5. Use word groups or full names whenever you can. You may need to enclose them in quotation marks, like "George W. Bush" or "Orlando wetlands sewage treatment." (More details about quotation marks a bit later.)
6. Use symbol or Boolean operators. (Details about these below.)
7. If your search engine offers the option, do a second search *within* the sites you've already found.

These seven strategies will help limit the number of hits, so the matches you get will be more relevant to your focused topic.

Fourth Principle: Retry the Search

If you type in a keyword, ask your search engine to find it, and get no hits, what's next?

1. Check spelling. Generally, the computer doesn't recognize nearly correct spelling, only exactly correct, although some search engines will ask "Did you mean . . ." if it senses a nearly correct misspelling.

CRITICAL THINKING HINT

Many words have more than one accepted spelling, especially in other parts of the English-speaking world. Since the Web is global, the alternate spellings may be an issue, depending of course on your topic. For instance, compare these accepted alternate spellings: *theater, theatre; counseling, counselling; gray, grey; color, colour.* Think about your own topic. Are alternate spellings an issue?

2. Check your KWL chart and cluster map for other words. Look for synonyms.
3. Try combining fewer terms. Begin with one or two terms and then add one at a time.
4. Put important terms first. Instead of listing "flea collars, cats, pets," list "pets, cats, flea collars."

These four principles are major clues to solving the mystery of research on the Net. Put them to work as you conduct your search.

SYMBOL AND BOOLEAN OPERATORS

Symbol operators tell the search engine how to use the words in your keyword search. They let you tell the search engine to use whole phrases, to exclude certain words, and to find words that should appear close together. Here's how the symbol operators work:

- Quotation marks (" ") show most search engines that they should find the whole phrase.
  Example: "Challenger explosion" (finds only sites including both words)
- A plus sign (+) in front of a word means it must appear in the pages.
  Example: iceberg +Newfoundland (finds pages about icebergs that also include the word "Newfoundland")
- A minus sign (–) in front of a word means it must not appear in the pages.
  Example: iceberg –Greenland (finds pages about icebergs, but *not* pages that also include the word "Greenland")

TECH TIP

Be sure to leave a space in front of the plus or minus sign but no space between it and the next word, like this: "wood +preservative."

- An asterisk (*) in the middle of a word, called a **wildcard**, tells the search engine to find related words.
  Example: g*se (searches for "goose" and "geese")
- An asterisk (*) at the end of a word, called **truncation**, tells the search engine to find a whole group of words.
  Example: invest* (finds "investment," "investing," "investigator," "invested," "investigating," "investigation," and any of the plural forms, like "investigations" or "investments")
- The word "title" or just "t" followed by a colon restricts your search to only titles containing your keyword.
  Example: t:money (finds all documents with "money" in their titles)

Boolean operators, named after the logician who created the form, are words (always in all capital letters) that help define your search. Here are the common words.

- AND is used like + and tells the search engine to find all words connected with AND.
  Example: Thomas AND Jefferson AND president (results in all three words anywhere on the page)

CRITICAL THINKING HINT

The more terms you hook together with AND, the fewer the hits you'll get. It's a great way to reduce 63,492 hits to 79 and get more precise—and more relevant—results. Here are some hints: You can put together several important terms with the word. Remember your cluster map and all the words you found related to your topic? Put some of the important ones together with AND and see what happens.

- OR expands a search.
  Example: Jefferson OR president (finds any reference to any Jefferson and any reference to any president, maybe even president of the local Chamber of Commerce)

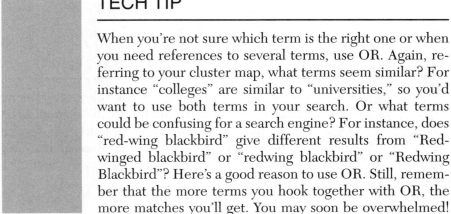

TECH TIP

When you're not sure which term is the right one or when you need references to several terms, use OR. Again, referring to your cluster map, what terms seem similar? For instance "colleges" are similar to "universities," so you'd want to use both terms in your search. Or what terms could be confusing for a search engine? For instance, does "red-wing blackbird" give different results from "Red-winged blackbird" or "redwing blackbird" or "Redwing Blackbird"? Here's a good reason to use OR. Still, remember that the more terms you hook together with OR, the more matches you'll get. You may soon be overwhelmed!

- ANDNOT will eliminate certain terms in a search.
  Example: Jefferson ANDNOT movie (finds all references to any Jefferson, but not those pages that are movie reviews)

- NEAR will find terms within 10 spaces of each other.
  Example: Thomas NEAR Jefferson (finds the two names within 10 spaces)
- Any combination of these terms will result in an even more refined search.
  Example: Thomas AND Jefferson NEAR president ANDNOT book (gets fairly complex but eliminates lots of useless results about some other Thomas Jefferson or book reviews)

TECH TIP

Remember that Boolean operators must appear in all capital letters and that there must be a space before and after the operating word.

- Parentheses ( ) allow you to use several operators at once, but be careful where you put the parentheses. Compare these examples:
  Examples: (Thomas OR Tom) AND Jefferson (finds any Jefferson whose first name is written either as Thomas or Tom)
  Tom OR (Thomas AND Jefferson) (finds references to any Tom and also any references to Thomas Jefferson—probably not what you really want)

TECH TIP

Once you use a Boolean operator, the relevance ranking may no longer be in effect. You'll need to skim all or at least most of the results instead of just the first several dozen. At the same time, of course, the Boolean operator will significantly reduce the number of hits you will have available to skim.

You may be left with one question: How do you know when to use which? Two hints:

- Use quotation marks for specific events, places, or names that frequently are used together:

Examples: "George W. Bush"
"World Trade Center"
"World Series"
- Use AND for less commonly joined words or phrases:
Examples: George AND Bush AND Texas
World AND Trade AND Center AND bombing
2001 AND World AND Series

CRITICAL THINKING HINT

Notice that the use of certain symbols and certain Boolean terms will give the same results. Why have more than one way to do something? Remember that search engines do not all operate the same way. If a symbol operator works on one, perhaps the Boolean operator does not. Try everything that makes sense.

Depending on how comfortable you are with all the details about using search engines (in the generic sense), you may want to explore some further details.

Remember that every search engine has its own Help button. Whether it's called "Help," "Search Tips," "Advanced Search," or something else, there you can find details about what this search engine can and can't do. Let's say you want to know about the search engine you're using and whether it

- covers newsgroups
- lets you do symbol operator searches
- lets you do Boolean operator searches, and what kinds
- lets you ask for a search that must, should, or could include certain terms
- allows you to limit your search to a geographic region
- searches differently with and without capital letters
- will automatically find the plural, infinitive, or present participle form of your search word

Answers to these and other questions are only a click away—all clues to solving the research mystery! Use your search engine's Help button regularly!

TECH TIP

Know your search engine's peculiarities. Some are case sensitive. That means they know the difference between upper- and lowercase letters. So if you ask for "bill clinton," it will search for anything about "bill," including the one you get from the electric company. If you ask for "Bill Clinton," it will search for only those capitalized words.

CRITICAL THINKING HINT

Remember to think along the lines of "What if I try . . ." For instance, try changing the order of the words in your search phrase. If you don't get the results you hoped for when you asked for "bluebird nest cavities," ask for "cavity nest bluebirds" or "bluebird cavity nest."

Finally, some search engines will let you look for "More Like This" or "Search These Results." Both allow you to refine your search and further limit the number of irrelevant sites.

CRITICAL THINKING HINT

If you study the search engine home pages carefully, you'll find a couple that allow you to "Ask the Expert." Believe it or not, you'll get a real person, an expert in his or her field, who will e-mail you a personal response to a specific question. If you're required to include primary research in your report, you'll discover a real gold mine here!

EVALUATING WEB SITES

By now you've found numerous useful sites that are directly related to your working outline. All you need to do is gather the information and put it in your report, and you're home free. Wrong, wrong, wrong! Here's why.

Not all parts of the Web are created equal. Anybody can publish anything on the Web. Miss Minnie's first-grade class can post a site on nuclear physics as easily as can a Nobel Prize winner. In fact, frustrated writers who can't find a reputable, legitimate publishing house to print their work in book or periodical form frequently turn to the Web to publish their thoughts. No one edits the Web. No one demands honesty on the Web. No one demands legitimacy on the Web.

In short, as a researcher, you are entirely responsible for determining what is and what is not legitimate, accurate information coming off the Web. How do you know? Well, there are no hard-and-fast rules, but there are four reasonably sound guidelines—more clues to solving the research mystery.

GUIDELINE 1: CHECK OUT THE URL ENDING

Start by checking the URL ending. The ending tells you something about the site's sponsor. Here is a list of the most common URL endings:

.com = a commercial company
.net = usually a communications provider or foreign site
.org = an organization, usually but not always nonprofit, always with
    a mission
.gov = a governmental institution, local, state, or federal
.edu = an educational institution, private or public, from elementary
    school through university
.mil = a branch of the military

CRITICAL THINKING HINT

Think about what the URL ending may mean about a site. A commercial site may be shortlived, while an educational or governmental site is likely to be fairly stable. In addition, think about biases. For instance, if it's ".org," what may this organization be trying to promote? Most likely, the information at an organization's **Web address** will be biased toward whatever it tries to promote.

Think about the various URL endings. If the ending is ".org," you can make some assumptions about the site. For instance, if you're looking at the National Wildlife Conservation organization's site, you're not likely to find details on how to drain a wetland. That action is contrary to the organization's purpose. On the other hand, an organization nationally recognized for its research may be the most reputable site for your topic. For instance, the American Cancer Society is an organization that sponsors cancer research. Thus, at their site you may find not only up-to-date research results but also links to other reputable cancer/health sites.

What general statements apply to ".gov," ".edu," and ".mil" sites? Certainly ".gov" sites are great for statistics about any local, state, or federal issue. And since every department or bureau usually has its own part of the Web site, you can find volumes of information. Usually the sites focus on factual information. Much the same can be said about ".mil" sites. Still, keep in mind that they are detailing information from their perspective. For instance, government sites present details in terms of the government (and probably political) point of view.

TECH TIP

Glitzy sites often attract the most attention. They appeal to your visual excitement and aim to woo Web browsers into their lair. Be careful! Glitzy doesn't necessarily mean accurate. In fact, sometimes the fancy graphics and other bells and whistles cover up a real lack of content. Likewise, you may find sites (especially those ending in ".com") with so much fancy advertising that it overtakes editorial space. In that case, question the site's validity. Have the advertisers dictated what can and cannot appear on the site? Or does the site exist in order to advertise? Be wary! Judge Web content on its own terms, not the way it's packaged and presented.

Sites with URLs ending in ".edu" can be profoundly helpful. Keep in mind, however, that you're likely to find lots of class outlines or individual lesson outlines posted by teachers and professors. You may even find student work posted on elementary, middle, or high school sites, or a university student can have a page that is not necessarily sanctioned by a university. Still, once you sift out the class guides, lesson outlines, and student pages, you'll find that most universities have truly fine sites loaded with powerful information. There's a simple reason for that: Professors who devote their academic lives to a given subject often post their research results or in-depth discussions of at least the important aspects of their subjects at their university's Web site. So when your search engine turns up a ".edu" site, do take notice of its source and content.

GUIDELINE 2: CHECK RELEVANCY

After you've checked the URL ending, what else can you do to figure out if a site is suitable for your use? Redirect your focus on the writing process. Two key questions will help you zero in on your next step. Ask yourself:

1. Is the information relevant?
2. Does it address what my assignment asks me to do?

Your search engine will likely turn up dozens of sites that on the surface seem to have something to do with your focused topic. A closer look may reveal that they are only indirectly related, maybe very indirectly related.

CRITICAL THINKING HINT

As you skim through the site, make sure you're not being led astray. Although the information may be interesting, if it does not deal directly with your focused topic, move on. What's the best test? Ask yourself this question: Does this site answer a question on my KWL chart? If not, go elsewhere—now!

GUIDELINE 3: CHECK THE HOME PAGE

Assuming you have found a site with information relevant to your topic, how do you figure out if the site is reputable? Go to the Web site's home page. The home page is somewhat like a book's title page, table of contents, index, and introduction all rolled into one. It's also the place where you'll find answers to many of the questions you should ask yourself about any Web site.

TECH TIP

Generally your search engine won't take you to a site's home page. Instead, it takes you to the page where your keywords appear. Somewhere on that page, however, you should find a button labeled "Home," and clicking there will take you to the site's home page. Or if there is no home page, go to the root of the URL, to the ".com," ".org," or other ending.

Here are a half dozen questions you need to ask:

1. Who wrote the material on the Web site? Is the author's or **Web master's** name and e-mail and/or postal address listed on the site?
   - Unless you're searching an organization's Web site (".org"), you should find an author's or Web master's name, e-mail, and/or postal address. Otherwise, you should view the site with caution. Anyone worth reading will be willing to be accountable for the content.
   - While e-mail and postal addresses may not interest you, an author hiding behind the Web has questionable motives for writing. Chances are, citing his or her words won't enhance your research report.

CRITICAL THINKING HINT

When you find an author's or Web master's e-mail address, you can write for a personal response to a particularly puzzling part of your research. These folks could, in fact, be the experts! Just be wary: Be sure you've made every effort to find the information elsewhere first so that you're not annoying the experts with what should be basic research. Second, check credentials—as always—to see if these folks really are the experts. More on that in the next point.

2. Is the author an authority on the subject? Has he or she written any other materials that have been published, either in hard copy or on the Web?

   - At the end of the Web site, you may find a bibliography citing other works by the author. Check them out. They can be helpful in your search for resources.
   - You can also do a keyword search of the author's full name to see what turns up. That search may uncover some really fine information for your report. Or you may learn that this author has no other credentials to his or her name.

3. Is there a list of works cited by the Web site author(s)?

   - Not only does a list of works cited add credibility to the Web site, it also gives you another means of finding resources. Check them out!

TECH TIP

Don't panic if a site lists no author. Study the home page. Sometimes you'll find a reference to a group, like a medical group or museum staff. That means that more than one person contributes to the site, usually in cooperation with a single Web master. If it's a university site, for instance, then each professor may have access to posting on the site. Think carefully about what you find on the home page before you throw up your hands over a lack of authorship.

4. Are there links to other sites?

   - Links to other similar sites can send you to valuable resources. If they seem logical and relevant to your focused topic, check them out.
   - Be sure to evaluate the links to see if you can spot any particular bias or special interest. Be careful if you find evidence of propaganda, like slanted writing, name-calling, or strong, nonobjective language. Be cautious of dead links.

5. Who is the sponsor of the Web site?

   - Sponsors are likely to be more responsible about their site's content than are independent service providers. Such sponsors include organizations, educational institutions, and governmental bodies. Independent service providers are primarily interested in the income they gain from posting the site. Check the URL ending to know.

- What is the sponsor's mission, statement of purpose, or list of objectives? If you don't find this information on the home page, it may appear elsewhere. Check the home page *site map* for buttons like "Contact us," "Who we are," "About us," or "History." Sponsorship will, in most cases, color what appears on a site. Just be aware.
- Is there an affiliation to a respected institution, like a university? The more respected the institutional affiliation, the more reputable the Web site is likely to be. But if there is no institutional affiliation apparent, don't panic. Other clues can help you decide the Web site's validity. Keep reading for more!

6. When was the site created and/or last updated?
   - A site created in 1994 that has not been updated since then may be too old to be acceptable. That depends, of course, on the subject matter and how much has changed in the past years.
   - An old site without any updates may represent an abandoned site that no one bothered to dismantle when its usefulness ended.
   - The date of the most recent update is usually given at the very bottom of the home page. If it's not there, and you find nothing else to indicate a creation date or update, check the copyright date. A recent copyright date (within the last year) suggests that the site is probably current.

GUIDELINE 4: SKIM THE SITE

Assuming you're comfortable with the authorship, sponsorship, and timeliness of the Web site, the next step is to skim the site for four clues about a Web site's credibility:

1. What is the site's purpose? Does it educate, entertain, inform, or promote someone or something?
   - As you skim through a site, you'll get a general idea of its purpose.

CRITICAL THINKING HINT

Every site has its own bias. The information you find at any given site will be filtered through the sponsor's best interests. For example, to be ridiculously obvious, you won't find Ford vehicles touted on a site sponsored by a Chevrolet dealer. Less obviously, perhaps, you won't find explanations about the pros and cons of logging state forests at state forest sites. So think carefully about the Web site's purpose and what it means about the information posted there.

- When a Web site requires that you make a donation or take some action (buy something, contact someone, subscribe to something), run like lightning. It's most likely not a reputable research site.

TECH TIP

Some sites ask you to register. More and more newspapers now require registration to access current articles, as do certain magazines and scholarly journals. Reputable sites have privacy policies the user can read and accept—or not—before registering. Use caution before giving any personal information online.

- As a researcher, you're looking for something designed to educate or inform, with biases understood.
2. Does the information reinforce or contradict what you found in print sources (books and/or periodicals)?
   - If the Web site reiterates what you've already found in print, skip it unless it offers something new. You don't need another summary or restatement of what you've read elsewhere.
   - If the Web site contradicts what you've found in print, question which is accurate. Delve into details about who the author is, where he or she gets information, and which source—print or the Web—is more current. Then consider whether the newer information is a logical extension of the old or whether it's really contradictory.

3. Do you find anything on the Web site worded exactly as you read it elsewhere?
   - If you find duplicate information, you've uncovered plagiarism, the act of stealing someone else's words and calling them your own. Unfortunately, some disreputable Web sites post plagiarized information. It amounts to literary theft. Avoid any site that even hints of plagiarism.
   - So who copied from whom? In general, when plagiarism is the issue, print sources tend to be more reputable than Web sites.
4. Is there more glitz than content on the Web site? Does the glitz try to distract you from the lack of depth of information?
   - While visuals add to a site's appeal, ask yourself why the author or sponsor found the appeal necessary.
   - Is the information inadequate without the visuals? Do the visuals in fact clarify the information? Or do the visuals actually seem to serve no purpose?
   - Don't judge a site by its cover!

These four guidelines should help you decide whether a site is credible and suitable for your research topic.

Finally, let's check out some common misunderstandings about your Web search.

1. A Web search is as comprehensive a search as you can make.
2. Whatever search tool worked best last time will work best this time.
3. When you decide on a search engine, there's no need to try other search tools.

If you think these are all true statements, you're in big trouble. In short, when you've finished your initial Web search, you're not finished searching. You should use a combination of resources.

- A subject index may send you to a keyword search through a search engine.
- A newsgroup may connect you with the experts' names whose books you can find in the library.
- A keyword search through a search engine may link you to a library catalog and take you to virtual library stacks.
- A Web search for current information may send you to a database for historical background.
- A directory search may take you to bibliographies.

CRITICAL THINKING HINT

How do you know when your Web search is finished? The due date for your project and how much other homework you have usually dictate when your search is finished. That's the practical response. But there's a better answer to the question. When you start getting the same information repeated or the same Web sites listed again and again, you know you've adequately explored the Web.

SAVING WEB RESEARCH

The Web changes hourly. A site is here today and gone tomorrow. The millions of sites face constant updates and deletes. No one anywhere could possibly keep track of the changes—including you! The site you found last night that seemed entirely reputable and perfect for your narrowed topic may be gone today. So what do you do when you find something really hot? Here are some suggestions.

1. Save the information on a disk, CD, or external storage media. Then you can be confident of its existence throughout your research time.
2. Use **bookmarks** to identify a site for future reference. Don't bookmark the home page; instead bookmark the specific page where you found great information. Then later you can return directly to the pertinent information. No wading through numerous steps from the home page or following a whole chain of links.
3. Print out the vital information. Then you can file those pages and refer to them at your leisure, even away from your computer. (Most computer systems print out the site's URL, either at the top or bottom of the page of text. Thus, you'll always know where each printed page came from.)

TECH TIP

Believe it or not, some students think they can print out whatever they find on the Web and turn it in as "their" report. Wrong, wrong, wrong! Whether you're doing research from hard copy or from the Web, you must, *absolutely must*, put your research into your own words and cite the sources where your information came from.

Be careful when you decide to print from a Web site. Always check "Print Preview" to see how many pages you'll be printing if you just hit the Print button. It's foolish to print 30 pages when you need only two. (And you'll find out with "Print Preview" that some Web pages are protected so that you can't print them out. The preview page shows a blank. Thus, you'll know there's nothing wrong with your printer or your **printer feed**.)

TIME MANAGEMENT GUIDELINES

Some students spend far too much time searching the Web for information. Rather, they should spend the bulk of their time searching the library and its resources, whether the resources are electronic or print. Thus, no matter how much time you have to complete your paper, we recommend no more than one day for Web searching.

Number of weeks to work on final paper	Number of days available to find Web resources
10	1
8	1
6	1
4	1

Two Students' Progress

Sarah and Terry faced very different situations in terms of Web research. While Sarah found some good information, Terry chose not to use the Web at all.

Sarah

I knew that certain organizations were active in supporting wetlands research and wetlands preservation, so I wanted to check their Web sites for any insights. Likewise, because my print sources made frequent references to the Environmental Protection Agency (EPA), I thought I should consult that site as well, perhaps for statistics or other historical and current details. But I also decided to do a keyword search just to see what showed up.

Using one search engine, I had 154 site matches, but who wants to take hours and hours to check that many sites? Using another search engine that gives results by relevancy, I had 6,016 hits with the keyword search "wetlands," but only the top 10 or 12 listings had 99% relevancy. I cruised through those and found a Wetlands Network home page with some good links. In turn, that connected me to some government agencies and national organizations— certainly more valid sites than some individual advocate's home page! I copied down the URLs so I could come back later, read more carefully, print out good sources, and use my time more productively.

All in all, I spent about a hour and a half at the keyboard.

Terry

I chose not to spend time searching the Web. Frankly, the assignment didn't seem to lend itself to that means of research.

Tips and Traps

Sarah offered two suggestions for using the Web for your research. First, she noted that the Web is a powerful source for finding other sources. At reputable Web sites, look for bibliographies, such lists perhaps being the most valuable research tool the site offers.

Keep in mind, too, that you can find online help for every search engine on the Web. Look on the search engine home page for links to the help screens. Directions are crystal clear. Follow them!

Finally, be warned that the Web should not be the primary source of your research. The following chart illustrates a suggested guide for the distribution of your resources. Your teacher may impose other guidelines.

Where will YOU find information for your class projects?

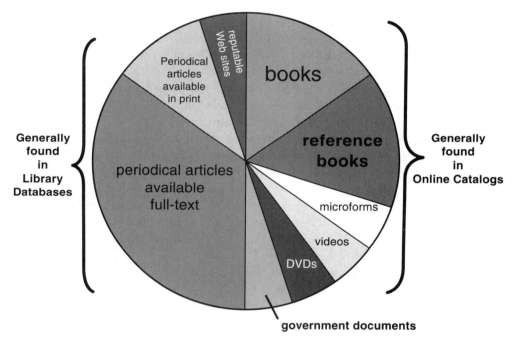

Created by Susan Metcalf, Instructional Services Librarian, USI

CHECKLIST FOR LOCATING AND EVALUATING WEB RESOURCES

You should be able to answer "yes" to the following questions about locating and evaluating your Web resources.

1. Have I used at least three search engines to make sure I found the best resources?

2. Did I narrow my search appropriately, using symbol and/or Boolean operators as necessary?
3. Did I try a variety of keywords and combinations of words and/or phrases to refine my search?
4. If my topic suggested, did I use directories and/or mega-search engines for additional results?
5. Have I skimmed the search results and accessed only the most promising sites?
6. Did I evaluate the sites based on the URL ending?
7. Did I evaluate the sites to determine if information there supported my working outline and/or answered questions from my KWL chart?
8. Did I evaluate the site by checking the home page to determine authorship and reliability?
9. Did I skim, rather than read in detail, the most promising sites to check for information that would support my working outline and/or answer questions from my KWL chart?
10. Have I bookmarked or otherwise saved sites with information supporting my working outline and/or my KWL chart for future reference?

EXERCISES

Exercise A: Using Search Engines

Directions: With a peer group, choose three keyword searches from among those listed below, or choose your own. Enter each into at least three search engines. Compare the results. What conclusions can you draw about the results?

Vietnam War	Gulf War
campaign finance	wetlands
John Steinbeck	wetlands preservation
Amish	terrorist
Amish culture	urban sprawl
Amish beliefs	ozone layer
Mars rover	election fraud

Exercise B: Using Symbol and Boolean Operators

Directions: Explain what results you would get by entering the following symbol and Boolean operators in a keyword search.

1. George Washington
2. "George Washington"
3. George +Washington
4. George –Washington
5. George AND Washington
6. George OR Washington
7. George NEAR Washington
8. George AND Washington NOT Carver

Exercise C: Evaluating Web Sites

Directions: Choose two of the following Web sites, or choose two sites of your own, and evaluate each according to what its URL tells you and according to information on its home page. (Review guidelines 1 and 3 for evaluating Web sites on pages 69 and 71.) Explain why the site would or would not be suitable as a resource.

www.nvf.org
www.audubon.org
www.nature.org
www.nasa.gov
http://stats.bls.gov
www.loc.gov
www.washingtonpost.com
www.cbsnews.com
www.pbs.org
www.weather.com

5

Preparing Bibliography Cards

Your library, online, and Web searches have put print and electronic resources in your hands. Your immediate task now is to develop a system by which to keep track of these materials—their titles, authors, publishers, dates of publication, page references, sources, etc. The best system is a set of bibliography cards, one card for each source. Alphabetized, bibliography cards become the Works Cited page at the end of the final paper.

You may argue, "What's there to keep track of? I have all the sources right here on my desk or bookmarked on my computer." True, at the moment you do, but library materials come due and must be returned, often before your paper is finished, and Web sites can change overnight. Aside from those little matters of inconvenience, however, you must also keep track of which information comes from which source so that you can accurately document your paper. Since documentation is one of the characteristics that distinguish a research paper from other papers, most educators cast a critical eye on all aspects of the documentation process. Thus, you need to put the system in operation and prepare a bibliography card for each of the sources you have collected. And you need to do it now, *before* you begin reading and taking notes.

By methodically and carefully preparing bibliography cards now, before you begin reading and taking notes, you will save hours of work later.

GENERAL GUIDELINES

The following suggestions will help you develop a clear, accurate set of bibliography cards. Following this list of general guidelines, you will find a complete set of sample bibliography forms in both the humanities style and the science style.

1 *Use bibliography cards of a different size or color from your note cards.* Some writers prefer 3″ × 5″ cards for the bibliography and 4″ × 6″ cards for notes; others prefer a pastel color for bibliography cards and white for note cards. To distinguish them by size or color is to keep from accidentally "losing" a bibliography card later among your many note cards.

2 *Use a separate card for each bibliography entry.* As part of your final manuscript, you will prepare an alphabetical list of works cited. With each resource listed on a separate card, you will be able to alphabetize easily. (See completed Works Cited pages in the model papers in Chapter 14.)

3 *Write in ink.* Pencil smears, and ultimately it may render an entry illegible.

4 *Be sure to list all necessary information.* For books, most information will be on the title and copyright pages. For magazines, most information will be on the front cover or on one of the first pages, like the table of contents page or the page listing the editorial staff. For online or Web resources, most information is on the opening or closing screen.

5 *Separate titles from subtitles.* If a book or magazine article title includes a subtitle, separate it from the main title by a colon. Follow this guideline no matter how the title and subtitle appear together in the book or magazine.

6 *For books, note the call number in the lower left corner of the card.* Always record the library call number of any book you use. If for some reason you need the book again later, you will be able to find it quickly without again searching the catalog.

7 *Record the library name.* If you get materials from more than one library, also record on each bibliography card the name of the library from which you obtained the reference. That information will prove invaluable in case you need to check some detail later.

8 *Make a note of any outstanding features.* Some sources will include special features like good charts, an extensive index, a bibliography, or good background. Others may be less impressive, perhaps too technical or include only a brief chapter. Making notes of such features will help you remember which sources initially seem most beneficial.

9 *Punctuate titles within titles correctly.* Consider these examples:

> (Book titles are shown here in italics but should be underlined in your manuscript.)

> "Imagery in F. Scott Fitzgerald's *The Great Gatsby*"
>   (article title including a book title)
> "Imagery in Robert Frost's 'Birches' "
>   (article title including a poem title)
> *Critical Reflections on* The Great Gatsby
>   (book title including another book title)
> *Imagery in "The White Heron"*
>   (book title including a short story title)

TECH TIP

You can easily record bibliography information on your computer. You may want to insert information alphabetically as you go. (See Chapter 12 for details about alphabetizing a list of works.)

Be sure to create a separate file for your list of bibliography references.

When you have finished entering the information, save it, but also print out a copy so you can refer to it quickly while taking notes. And remember to make a backup!

CONTENT AND FORM

Different kinds of sources—books, periodicals, Web pages—all require different forms for their respective bibliography cards. Even online periodicals have a different bibliography form than do periodicals in print. The business of correctly writing your bibliography cards is further complicated by the fact that there are two styles for each of these forms: a style used for the humanities and another used for the sciences. Use the style your teacher prefers.

What follows are generic directions and specific illustrations for creating either humanities-style or science-style bibliography cards for the sources most commonly used in research papers.

CRITICAL THINKING HINT

Keep in mind that no matter how thorough a list of examples is provided in this or any other style manual, you may find a source for which there is no specific example. In that case, use common sense to list the author, title, and publishing information in a manner consistent with the examples.

A final suggestion: pay careful attention to every comma, space, period, underscore, capital letter, and number. Writing accurate bibliography entries takes an eye for detail and attention to consistency.

Note: In addition to the examples below, see the model Works Cited and References pages for the student model papers in Chapter 14.

BOOKS

For a book, the humanities style bibliography form needs the following information:

1. Author(s) or editor(s), last name first, followed by a period
2. Title of book, underlined (or in italics, as your teacher directs), followed by a period
3. Publication information, including
   • Place of publication, followed by a colon
   • Publisher, followed by a comma
   • Date of publication (most recent), followed by a period
4. Arranged in hanging indentation form (all but the first line is indented)

Note that the science style bibliography form for a book

1. uses the author's last name but only initials for first and middle names.
2. encloses the date of publication in parentheses, followed by a period.
3. capitalizes only the first word and proper names in titles of books.

In order to cite a book found online, use the humanities and science styles for electronic sources, beginning on page 92.

Book by a Single Author

Humanities Style

> Benson, Jackson J. *The True Adventure of John Steinbeck, Writer.* New York: Penguin Books, 1984.

> _Thom, James Alexander. Long Knife: A Novel Based on the Life of George Rogers Clark_. New York: Ballantine Books, 1979.
>
> Thom also wrote _From Sea to Shining Sea_ about expedition (also fiction, history based) (county library)

Science Style

> Benson, J. J. (1984). *The true adventure of John Steinbeck, writer.* New York: Penguin Books.

Book by Two Authors

Note that the humanities-style bibliography form lists the second author's name in first-name-last-name order. Note that the science style maintains last name first for the second author and uses the ampersand (&) instead of the word "and."

Humanities Style

> Gielgud, John, and John Miller. *Acting Shakespeare*. New York: Charles Scribner's Sons, 1991.

Science Style

> Gielgud, J., & Miller, J. (1991). *Acting Shakespeare*. New York: Charles Scribner's Sons.

Book by Three Authors

Humanities Style

> Hirsch, E. D., Jr., Joseph F. Kett, and James Trefil. *The Dictionary of Cultural Literacy: What Every American Needs to Know*. 2d ed. Boston: Houghton Mifflin Company, 1993.

Science Style

> Hirsch, E. D., Jr., Kett, J. F., & Trefil, J. (1993). *The dictionary of cultural literacy: What every American needs to know*. 2d ed. Boston: Houghton Mifflin Company.

Book with Four or More Authors

Humanities Style

> Shepard, Alan, Deke Slayton, Jay Barbree, and Howard Benedict. *Moon Shot: The Inside Story of America's Race to the Moon*. Atlanta: Turner Publishing, Inc., 1994.

Science Style

> Shepard, A., Slayton, D., Barbree, J., & Benedict, H. (1994). *Moon shot: The inside story of America's race to the moon*. Atlanta: Turner Publishing, Inc.

Book with an Editor or Editors

Humanities Style

> Polking, Kirk, Joan Bloss, and Colleen Cannon, eds. *Writer's Encyclopedia*. Cincinnati: Writer's Digest Books, 1983.

Science Style

> Polking, K., Bloss, J., & Cannon, C. (Eds). (1983). *Writer's encyclopedia*. Cincinnati: Writer's Digest Books.

Work in an Anthology
Humanities Style

> Dove, Rita. "The Oriental Ballerina." *The Norton Anthology of African-American Literature*. Eds. Henry Louis Gates Jr., and Nellie Y. McKay. New York: W. W. Norton & Company, 1997.

Science Style

> Dove, R. (1997). The oriental ballerina. In H. L. Gates Jr., & N. Y. McKay (Eds.), *The Norton anthology of African-American literature* (pp. 117–123). New York: W. W. Norton & Company.

Multivolume or Translated Work
Humanities Style

> Prost, Antoine, and Gerard Vincent, eds. *A History of Private Life*. Vol. 5. Trans. Arthur Goldhammer. Cambridge: Harvard University Press, 1991.

Science Style

> Prost, A., & Vincent, G. (Eds.). (1991). *A history of private life*. (A. Goldhammer, Trans). Cambridge: Harvard University Press.

Edition of a Book
Humanities Style

> Grauer, Robert T., and Gretchen Marx. *Essentials of the Internet*. 3rd ed. Upper Saddle River, NJ: Prentice Hall, 2003.

Science Style

> Grauer, R. T., & Marx, G. (2003). *Essentials of the internet* (3rd ed.). Upper Saddle River, NJ: Prentice Hall.

Article in a Reference Book

Humanities Style

"Steinbeck, John." *Contemporary Authors.* 1968.

Science Style

Steinbeck, John. (1968). *Contemporary authors.*

Two notes about reference book bibliography entries:

1. Many reference book articles, especially those in encyclopedias, are signed, the name appearing at the end of the article. Sometimes only initials appear. In that case, the initials will correspond to authors listed either in the front matter or in the index. When articles are signed, include the author's name in the bibliography entry.
2. No page number is necessary for alphabetically arranged references like dictionaries and encyclopedias.

Government Publication

Humanities Style

United States Dept. of Labor. Bureau of Statistics. *Dictionary of Occupational Titles.* 8th ed. Washington, D.C.: GPO, 2003.

Science Style

United States Dept. of Labor, Bureau of Statistics. (2003). *Dictionary of occupational titles* (8th ed.). Washington, D.C.: U.S. Government Printing Office.

Book Without Stated Publication Information

Use the following abbreviations when publication information is not included in the book:

n.p.	no place of publication given OR no publisher given
n.d.	no date of publication given
n. pag.	no pagination given

Insert the abbreviation in the bibliography entry at the point at which full information would otherwise appear.

PERIODICALS

For periodicals, the humanities style for the bibliography form needs the following information:

1. Author(s), if given, last name first, followed by a period
2. Title of article, enclosed in quotation marks, with a period inside the final quotation marks
3. Title of periodical, underlined (or in italics, as your teacher directs)
4. Date of publication, written for newspapers in day-month-year order, with the name of the month abbreviated, followed by a colon
5. Page(s), followed by a period

For periodicals, the science style for the bibliography form follows these additional details:

1. For article titles, capitalizes only the first word of titles, first word of subtitles, and all proper nouns
2. Omits quotation marks around article title
3. For magazine, journal, and newspaper titles, capitalizes all words except articles and prepositions, unless they are first or last words in the title
4. Spells out the name of the month
5. Includes the volume number (if given), underlined (or in italics, as directed by your teacher), followed by a colon, followed by the issue number (if given), followed by a comma

In order to cite a magazine, newspaper, or other periodical found on-line, either as an electronic publication or as a periodical accessed through a database, follow the citation forms found in the section for electronic sources, beginning on page 92.

Article from a Magazine

Humanities Style

> Kemper, Steve. "Madidi: Bolivia's Spectacular New National Park." *National Geographic* Mar. 2000: 5–23.

Science Style

> Kemper, S. (2000). Madidi: Bolivia's spectacular new national park. *National Geographic 194:* March 3, 5–23.

Unsigned Magazine Article

Humanities Style

> "Active Traveler Directory." *Outside* July 1997: 149–157.

Science Style

> Active traveler directory. (1997). *Outside*, July, 149–157.

Signed Newspaper Article

Humanities Style

> Johnson, Ella. "Legislators Rap Agency for Inaction." *Evansville Courier and Press*, 22 Apr. 2004: A5.

Science Style

> Johnson, E. (2004). Legislators rap agency for inaction. *Evansville Courier and Press*, 22 April, A5.

ELECTRONIC SOURCES

For electronic sources, the humanities-style bibliography form needs the following:

1. Author(s) or editor(s), if given, followed by a period
2. Title of page, in quotation marks, followed by a period
3. Title of site, underlined (or in italics, as your teacher directs), followed by a period
4. Date of publication or last update, with the name of the month abbreviated, followed by a period
5. Name of any institution or organization that sponsors the site (usually appears at the bottom of the site's home page), followed by a period
6. Date on which you accessed the page, with the name of the month abbreviated
7. The URL address, enclosed in angle brackets, followed by a period

TECH TIP

Citing online sources can be maddening since there is no consistency in what information appears online, either among databases or among Web sites. Thus, when you need additional examples, do a keyword search for "MLA style" if you're following the humanities style or "APA style" if you're following the science style. Check the constantly updated models from any of the many university sites your search turns up.

The science-style bibliography form for electronic sources

1. follows the date with a period, followed by the word "Retrieved" followed by the date you accessed the site (in month-day-year order, with the name of the month spelled out), followed by a comma, followed by the name of any organization or institution that sponsors the site (if given), followed by a colon
2. if no sponsor for the site is given, follows the date with a comma and the word "from" followed by the URL
3. omits the angled brackets around the URL

TECH TIP

If the URL must be divided between two lines of print, break it only after a slash. Do not add a hyphen at the break.

If the URL is extremely long, give the address of the site's search page. The shortened address helps avoid transcription errors, and the search page allows your reader to find the information using other publication facts in your citation.

An Entire Web Site

Humanities Style

> *Food and Nutrition Information Center.* 2004. National Agricultural Library, Division of the United States Department of Agriculture and Agricultural Research Service. 28 Apr. 2004 <http:www.nal.usda.gov/fnic>.

Bartleby.com: Great Books Online. Ed. Steven van Leeuwen. 2002. 28 Apr. 2004 <http://www.bartleby.com/>.

The Internet Public Library. 2004. The Regents of the University of Mich. School of Information. 28 Apr. 2004 <http://www.ipl.org/div/subject/browse/hum60.60.00/>.

Science Style

Food and nutrition information center. (2004). Retrieved April 28, 2004, from National Agricultural Library, Division of the United States Department of Agriculture and Agricultural Research Service site: http://www.nal.usda.gov/fnic.

Leeuwen, S. van. (Ed). (2002). *Bartleby.com: great books online.* Retrieved April 28, 2004, from http://www.bartleby.com/.

The Internet public library. (2004). Retrieved April 28, 2004, from The Regents of the University of Mich., School of Information site: http://www.ipl.org/div/subject/browse/hum60.60.00/.

A Signed (or Unsigned) Page within a Web Site

Note: For unsigned Web pages, use the following forms, only omitting the author name.

Humanities Style

DeWeerdt, Sarah. "Reflections on the Pond." *Conservation in Practice Online.* 2004 Winter. Society for Conservation Biology. 23 Apr. 2004 <http://www.conservationnews.org>.

Hajela, Deepti. "Teen Author Writes Best-Seller." CBSNews.com. 21 Apr. 2004. CBS Broadcasting, Inc. 21 Apr. 2004 <http://www.cbsnews.com/stories>.

Science Style

DeWeerdt, S. (2004, Winter). Reflections on the pond. *Conservation in Practice Online.* Retrieved April 28, 2004, from Society for Conservation Biology site: http.www.conservationnews.org.

A *Signed (or Unsigned) Article in* an Online Periodical

Note: For an unsigned article, use the following form, only omitting the author name.

Humanities Style

Johnson, Kirk. "Weapons Moving Out, Wildlife Moving In." *New York Times on the Web.* 23 Apr. 2004 <http://www.nytimes.com/pages/science/earth/index.html>.

Fording, Laura. "Education, 21st Century-Style." *Newsweek* 30 Mar. 2004. 23 Apr. 2004 <http://www.msnbc.msn.com/id/4633126>.

Science Style

Johnson, K. (2004). Weapons moving out, wildlife moving in. *New York Times on the Web.* Retrieved April 28, 2004, from http://www.nytimes.com/pages/science/earth/index.html.

Fording, L. (2004, March 30). Education, 21st century-style. *Newsweek.* Retrieved April 23, 2004, from http://www.msnbc.msn.com/id/4633126.

Note: For unsigned articles, use the same form, only omitting the author name.

Online Government Publication

Humanities Style

United States Department of Justice. Office of Juvenile Justice and Delinquency Prevention. *Detention and Juvenile Crime Repetition.* By Constance Conway. Sept. 2000. 14 May 2004 <http://www.ncjrs.org/pdffiles1/ojjdp/192245.pdf>.

Science Style

> Conway, C. (2000, September). Detention and juvenile crime repetition. United States Department of Justice, Office of Juvenile Justice and Delinquency Prevention. Retrieved May 14, 2004, from http://www.ncjrs.org/pdffiles1/ojjdp/192245.pdf.

Signed and Unsigned *Sources from* Library Subscription Services

Generally, you access databases through your library's subscription services by either using a computer terminal at the facility, like your school or neighborhood library, or entering a password at some other terminal, perhaps even in your own home. Since you likely found many of your resources through a database that your school or public library subscribes to, this section deserves special attention.

TECH TIP

Some common subscription services include EBSCOhost, Infotrac, Academic ASAP, NewsBank Info Web, SIRS (Social Issues Resources Series), and Proquest. Each subscription service employs a number of databases. Some of the common databases include MAS Ultra, Newspaper Source, ERIC, MasterFile Select, TOPIC search, Health Source, and Academic Search Elite.

If in the course of doing your research it isn't obvious to you which subscription services and which databases you are using, ask your librarian or media specialist.

In general, the humanities bibliography form for sources obtained through your library subscription services should include the following:

1. Author(s), if given, followed by a period
2. Title of the article, in quotation marks, followed by a period, with the period inside the final quotation marks
3. Title of the periodical or other source, underlined (or in italics, as your teacher directs)
4. Date of publication of the source, followed by a colon, followed by the page number(s), followed by a period
5. Name of the database through which you found the information

6. Name of the subscription service through which you accessed the database
7. Name of the library subscribing to the subscription service
8. Date you accessed the information
9. URL through which you accessed the information (probably the library's Web page)

The science bibliography form for sources attained through your library subscription services

1. includes the volume number, if given, following the title of the periodical or other source, underlined (or in italics, as your teacher directs), followed by a colon and the page number (not underlined or in italics), followed by a period
2. uses the word "Retrieved" followed by the date you accessed the site (in month, day, year order), followed by a comma
3. follows the access date with the word "from," followed by the name of the database.
4. does not include the subscription service, location from which you accessed the information, or URL of access site

Humanities Style

Covault, Craig. "Skycrane Reassessed." *Aviation Week and Space Technology* 22 Apr. 2004: 30. *Academic Search Elite.* EBSCOhost. Evansville Public Lib. 23 Apr. 2004 <http://www.evpl.org>.
"The Only Way Is Up." *New Scientist* 2 Nov. 2002: 176. *MasterFILE Premier.* EBSCOhost. Evansville Public Lib. 23 Apr. 2004 <http://www.evpl.org>.

Evans, Julie A. "Good Old-Fashioned Fitness." <u>Prevention</u> May 2004: 60. <u>Academic Search Elite</u>. EBSCO. Evansville Public Lib. 23 Apr. 2004 <http://www.evpl.org>.

refers to Old Order Amish—hard work, no obesity

Science Style

Covault, C. (2004, April 22). Skycrane reassessed. *Aviation Week and Space Technology, 160*, 30. Retrieved April 23, 2004, from Academic Search Elite Database.

The only way is up. (2002, November 2). *New Scientist, 176*: 40. Retrieved April 23, 2004, from MasterFILE Premier Database.

Material on CD-ROM

Humanities Style

Weeks, Sally, and George R. Parker. *Trees of Indiana: Their Identification and Uses.* CD-ROM. West Lafeyette, IN: Purdue University, 2002.

Science Style

Weeks, S., & Parker, G. R. (2002). *Trees of Indiana: Their identification and uses.* Retrieved from CD-ROM, Purdue University.

E-Mail Communication

Humanities Style

Goodaker, Donald. "Prodigal Returns." E-mail to the author. 30 Apr. 2004.

Science Style

Goodaker, D. (2004, April 30). "Prodigal returns." E-mail to the author.

OTHER PRINT AND NONPRINT RESOURCES

Pamphlet

Humanities Style

Online Scams: Potholes on the Information Highway. Washington, D.C.: FTC Bureau of Consumer Protection, Office of Consumer and Business Education, Mar. 1996.

Science Style

> *Online scams: Potholes on the information highway.* (1996, March). FTC Bureau of Consumer Protection, Office of Consumer Business Education.

Radio or Television Program

Humanities Style

> *Latest Edition.* Writ. Laura Lexter. PBS. WJXT, Princeton, 18 Sept. 2004.

Science Style

> Lexter, L. (2004, September 18). *Latest Edition.* PBS. WJXT, Princeton.

TIME MANAGEMENT GUIDELINES

Since you should prepare a bibliography card as soon as you find each source, suggesting a specific number of days for completing the task seems unnatural. If you prepare each card when you select the resource, you will hardly notice the time required. Perhaps the best advice is to add the following number of days to the time allotted for finding secondary sources:

Number of weeks to work on final paper	Number of days available to prepare bibliography cards
10	1
8	1
6	1
4	1

TWO STUDENTS' PROGRESS

Preparing bibliography cards offered different problems for Sarah and Terry. Compare their stories.

Sarah

I began writing out my bibliography cards as soon as I found the first few sources. Some sources seemed more useful than others, so I made brief notes on the cards about key points. For instance, some had good indexes, some were very brief, others had bibliographies of related sources.

I'll have to admit right now that I ended up not using all my sources. Some that I thought looked really good at first didn't offer much detail to support my outline. I found 34 sources— books, magazines, newspapers, computerized data sources, pamphlets—and I made a bibliography card for every one. I ended up taking notes from 29 and actually using 21 my paper. It was good to have those additional resources, though, in case I needed them to support some point in my outline I'd somehow overlooked.

Here's a shortcoming that cost me plenty of time later: I was sloppy with some of my bibliography cards and left out some things. For one magazine, I forgot to note the page numbers for the article I wanted to use. I didn't catch my error until later, after I'd returned my materials to the library. And guess what? Someone had already checked out that magazine again, so I had to go to a different library to get the information. What a waste of time! And all because of carelessness.

Terry

I had only four bibliography entries to write, so my job was a snap. Besides, I had done Works Cited pages last year and knew the ropes. In fact, I put my bibliography entries directly into the computer and never prepared individual cards. But let me tell you what happened to me and most of my classmates last year. When our teacher checked our bibliography cards, we had all made some silly mistakes—omitted commas, capitalized incorrectly, forgotten quotation marks or underscores, used incorrect spacing, substituted commas for periods—all kinds of little mechanical things. That was a clue that we'd better be as careful about those little details in bibliography entries as we are about mechanical details in our paragraphs! Having learned that lesson well, this year's work with bibliography form was a snap!

Tips and Traps

Most students face minor obstacles preparing bibliography cards. There are really only two requirements: (1) provide complete information and (2) consistently use the proper form. Meeting both requirements will assure an accurate Works Cited page in the final paper. More important, preparing the bibliography cards is the first step in accurate documentation. Since documentation is what sets the research paper apart from other papers, most teachers who assign a research paper want to see accurate, complete documentation. Work accordingly!

CHECKLIST FOR BIBLIOGRAPHY CARDS

You should be able to answer "yes" to each of these questions about each of your completed bibliography cards. (Questions are based on the humanities-style documentation form.)

1. Did I begin the first line of the bibliography entry at the left margin and indent all subsequent lines five spaces?
2. If the book or article has an author listed, have I begun each card with the author's name, written last name first, followed by a comma and the first name and, if given, the middle initial? If the book or article is unsigned, have I begun with the title?
3. Have I listed all titles correctly?
   a. Have I underlined titles of books, periodicals, and Web sites?
   b. Have I enclosed in quotation marks the titles of articles or Web pages?
   c. Did I capitalize words in titles correctly?
   d. Did I separate titles from subtitles with a colon?
4. Did I include all necessary publishing information for books?
   a. Did I list the place of publication?
   b. Did I follow the place of publication with a colon, a space, and the name of the publisher?
   c. Did I follow the name of the publisher with a comma and the date of publication?
5. Did I include all necessary publishing information for magazines?
   a. Did I follow magazine titles with the issue date?
   b. Did I list dates in the correct manner, listing first the day of the month, then the month, and then the year?

    c. Did I follow the date with a colon, a space, and the page number?

    d. Did I omit commas between the month and the year?

    e. Did I abbreviate the names of months correctly?

    f. Where I needed to name a state to identify the place of publication, did I use the two-letter abbreviation?

6. Did I include all necessary information for electronic sources?

    a. Did I cite the author or editor, if given?

    b. Did I include the title of the online page?

    c. Did I name the title of the Web site?

    d. Did I provide the last update or copyright date?

    e. Did I list the name of any sponsorship of the site?

    f. Did I give the date on which I accessed the site?

    g. Have I included the URL address, enclosed in angled brackets?

7. For sources accessed through library subscription services, did I include all necessary information for both the subscription service and the database(s) used?

    a. Did I list the author(s), if given?

    b. Did I give the title of the article?

    c. Did I give the title of the periodical or other source?

    d. Did I include the date of publication and page number of the source?

    e. Have I named the database through which I found the material?

    f. Have I named the subscription service through which I accessed the database?

    g. Did I name the library subscribing to the service used?

    h. Did I include the date on which I accessed the database?

    i. Have I included the URL through which I accessed the subscription service (probably the library's Web site)?

8. Have I used periods correctly?

    a. Have I followed each item (author name, article title, book title, and publishing information) with a period?

    b. Did I use only one period when the author's middle initial is included?

    c. Did I omit the period after magazine titles?

    d. Did I use a period at the end of each bibliography entry?

9. Did I include helpful information for myself?

    a. If I used more than one library, did I list the name of the library where I found this source?

    b. For books, did I list the call number?

    c. Did I make a brief notation about important features for key references?

10. Above all, am I consistent with all matters of style, using the same abbreviations, same format, same punctuation style, and same capitalization style throughout all of my bibliography cards?

EXERCISES

Exercise A: *Revising Bibliography Entries*

Directions: The following bibliography entries contain numerous mechanical errors. Rewrite them correctly in the humanities style.

Malcolm F. Baldwin. "Wetlands, Fortifying Federal and regional cooperation," *Environment*, September 1987: 16–20+.

Berle, Peter A. A. "The Audubon View: a grand Design for Wetlands" *Audubon*. July, 1990: 6.

"Nearly half Extinct Species were in Hawaii," April 23, 2004. <http://www.abcnews.go.com/wire/us/ap20040423_328html. *ABC News online*.

"Big Fault, no Blame," *Science* (Feb. 2002). 13:10. MasterFILE Premier. EBSCOhost. Mt. Vernon Public lib. Apr. 29, 2004. <www.mvpl.org>.

Easterbrook, Gregg "Cleaning Up" Newsweek. 24 July, 1989. pp. 26–42.

Goodwin, Richard H. and William A. Niering. *Inland Wetlands of the United States: Evaluated as potential registered natural landmarks*. New London, Conn., GPO. 1975.

Kusler, Jon A. "Our National Wetland Heritage: A Protection Guidebook". Washington. Environmental Law Institute. 1983.

Poole, Keith. Personal interview, April 29, 2004.

Exercise B: *Preparing Bibliography Cards*

Directions: Use the following information to prepare five bibliography cards. Use accurate form.

Sarah has found the following resources in two libraries. At the Vanderburgh County Library, she found two resources by William A. Niering. One is a book titled *Wetlands: The Audubon Society Nature Guides*. It was published in 1985 by Alfred A. Knopf in New York. The other is on CD-ROM from *The New Grolier Electronic Encyclopedia* published in Danbury, Connecticut, in 2004 by Grolier Electronic Publishing, Inc. The article is titled "Swamp, Marsh, and Bog."

At her school library, Sarah found one unsigned and two signed magazine articles. The unsigned article is in the November 2001 issue of *Southern Living* (pages 62, 66, and 68) and titled "Wetlands Ducks: The Timeless Equation." The other two articles are in the same July 1999 issue of *Audubon* magazine. One, by Peter Steinhart, is titled "No Net Loss" and is on pages 18–21. The other, titled "Symbols of the Marsh," is by George Reiger and appears on pages 52–58. She found all three of these on the MasterFILE Premier database through the Infotrac subscription service. Using her password, she accessed the database on April 30, 2004, through her school's (West Terrace High School) Web site: www.westterracehs.org.

Seeking Primary Resources

6

By no means does every research paper require primary references; however, most papers benefit from them. Primary resources lend personal anecdotes to impersonal research, add local color to broad issues, and show citizen response to controversies.

This chapter makes three assumptions:

1. You will be seeking primary and secondary resources simultaneously.
2. Your working outline will guide both searches.
3. Your searches will enhance your understanding and appreciation of your topic.

IDENTIFYING PRIMARY RESOURCES

Primary resources are those firsthand sources of someone's original words. Typically, they fall into two categories:

1. original works to which you are responding
2. original works that you create

You may be asked to write a paper in response to a literary work like a novel, poem, play, essay, or short story. Those literary works are primary sources—original works to which you are responding. Likewise, if you are writing about the Declaration of Independence, then that document is a primary source, as would be a newspaper interview or letter written at the time of the document's creation. There is little else we need say about those primary sources except to use them as your purpose and topic suggest.

The second category of primary sources, those you create yourself, need additional attention. They include, but are not limited to, the following:

1. interviews you conduct
2. letters written to you in response to your questions and prompts
3. experiments that you conduct or help conduct
4. surveys that you plan and carry out

Assuming that you want (or have been assigned) to incorporate primary research in your paper, this chapter will examine these four kinds of primary research and offer suggestions for your successful use of them.

As you work, keep in mind two general guidelines:

1. In order to create good primary resources, you need to have read widely enough about your topic in your secondary resources to ask intelligent questions, plan logical and relevant surveys, design successful experiments, and/or write meaningful letters.
2. Because primary research usually requires time from others (e.g., responding to interviews, letters, and surveys), be absolutely certain that you do not needlessly impose on others. Primary resources are *not* a substitute for reading and studying what the printed resources have to offer.

INTERVIEWS

Personal and telephone interviews are probably the most frequent forms of primary research for beginning research paper writers. The art of interviewing, however, requires careful preparation. Use the following steps to conduct your own interviews.

Preparing for the Interview

Step 1: *Read before you plan an interview.* Read enough of your secondary resources to know what you need to ask and of whom you need to ask it. Do you need an expert in some field, like a chemist, union leader, pest control operator, champion gymnast, jazz musician, wildlife biologist, historian, sociologist, school board member, florist, zoo director, or politician? Do you want that person to express an opinion, represent the opposition, give personal anecdotes, share local history, offer how-to ad-vice, share insights? What can this person provide that is not available in printed resources?

CRITICAL THINKING HINT

Most students overlook the vast community resources avail-able to them as primary sources. Think about your topic and who might be familiar with it or know someone who is.

Consider three examples:

Evan is researching what progress is being made in accurately predict-ing earthquakes, so he called the geology professor at a local college and was able to get the names of two leading seismologists, one of whom he was able to interview by telephone.

Danielle is comparing the outcomes of war criminal trials after World War II, so she talked to a neighbor who gave her the name of a member of the local German Heritage Club. That person in turn gave her the name of someone who had kept a scrapbook of German newspaper clippings about the trials. Danielle called for and was granted an interview. Al-though it took four phone calls and some added time on her part, the in-terview made a significant contribution to Danielle's paper.

Shanna is evaluating Kenya's most famous natural resource, its wildlife, as it affects the world economy, so she called the local travel bureau asking for names of recent visitors there. After seeking permission from its clients, the travel agent gave Shanna two names, one of whom was happy to talk with her about his three-week visit in Kenya's wildlife preserves. In addition, he gave her the name and e-mail address of an acquaintance who helped manage one of the preserves. Shanna could then write for answers to specific questions.

In each case, by mentally making connections between topics and po-tential resources, these students were able to add an important dimension to their research.

Step 2: *Arrange an interview time.* Professionals are busy people, and time is their most precious commodity. Whatever time you need will be time they must take from somewhere or someone else. Thus, when you call or write, be specific about:

1. who you are (identifying yourself and your school by name)
2. what you are doing (explaining that you are writing a research paper on a specific topic)

3. what you need (mentioning information about a specific issue)
4. how much time you need (identifying a specific time slot of 20 minutes, 30 minutes, an hour, etc.)

Ask for an appointment. Be prepared to conduct the interview at the interviewee's convenience, not yours. Agree on the specifics: date, time, place.

Remember, since you are asking for help, play the role of the Great Accommodator. If anyone is to be inconvenienced, it should be you. Do whatever you can to make the interview as nondisruptive to the interviewee's life as possible. You will get better results! As with any other pursuit, however, you should exercise sensible caution. For instance, be sure your teacher and parents or guardians know with whom, as well as when and where, you have scheduled your interview. And, of course, make sure they approve.

Step 3: Plan your questions. Your list of questions or issues will, of course, be guided by your working outline and your reading from secondary resources. Questions should be open-ended (i.e., without a simple right or wrong answer), should avoid a yes/no response, and should be focused enough to merit an answer suitable for use in your research paper.

Compare these questions based on Sarah's research topic:

1. How much of our nation's wetlands have been destroyed? (too specific for an interview; should have come from general reading)
2. In your opinion, what is the greatest problem in preserving the remaining wetlands? (good open-ended question; seeks up-to-date information)
3. Do you think it is important to save wetlands? (asks for a yes/no answer; leads nowhere in an interview)
4. What are the most important reasons for saving wetlands? (should have come from general reading)
5. How does the destruction of wetlands affect the average citizen in this community? (good open-ended question; allows local, personal response to an otherwise broad, impersonal issue)
6. What can citizens in this community do to protect wetlands? (gives opportunity for personal opinion; provides personal application to broad governmental rulings)

If you do not ask the right questions, you will not get the right information for your research.

By the way, there is one question you should always ask: "Can you recommend any particularly good books or articles on this topic?" That question gives you the opportunity to determine if you have already found the best sources or if you can profit by seeking others.

Step 4: Send a confirmation letter. Confirm by letter or by e-mail the date, time, and place of the interview. Include a list of general questions or issues you plan to address in the interview.

A confirmation serves two purposes. It reminds interviewees of their agreement to talk with you, and it helps them think about what you need. Some interviewees will even turn to their own primary sources for additional material if they know in advance you are seeking information not readily available to them.

On your own, prioritize the questions. If you run short of time during the interview, you may need to omit certain items. Identify the most important issues now.

TECH TIP

Prepare the confirmation letter using a computer and print two copies—one for the interviewee and one for you. Then you have two alternatives for prioritizing questions or concerns:

1. Insert numbers between paragraphs to indicate order of importance. You could also print out in bold or underline questions to make them highly visible for your own quick reading.
2. Rearrange the questions or concerns in the order in which you want to ask them.

Then print out a copy of your prioritized list, and you are ready for the interview!

Conducting the Interview

Step 5: Arrive early, properly dressed for the location. By arriving a few minutes early, you appear organized and professional. Of course, you must *never* keep an interviewee waiting—even though you may be (but should not be) kept waiting. Avoid jeans and T-shirt—unless you know the interviewee will be dressed the same way.

Step 6: Exchange pleasantries and begin the interview. Introduce yourself, be seated only when invited, establish rapport, remind your interviewee of your task at hand, maintain good eye contact, and begin with your first question or concern. Never interrupt. Do not chew gum. Do not drink or eat anything unless, of course, you are meeting at a restaurant.

CRITICAL THINKING HINT

Listen carefully to what your source is saying. Your task is to think, not talk. Think about his or her answers. What other questions do they raise? What unspoken ideas lie behind the words?

WARNING: Avoid plowing through your list of questions with such dogged determination that you miss new but important issues. Listen and think. Let each question build on the previous one.

Always keep in mind your specific topic, but remember that your working outline may not reflect every subtopic important to your research. Your interview may suggest new ones. Be ready to pursue new questions. At the same time, however, be sure to keep your interviewee on the subject.

Keep in mind the following suggestions as you question your interviewee. Think through these options before you leave one question and plow ahead thoughtlessly to another.

1. Respond with neutral expressions like "I see," "Yes," and "Uh-huh." These expressions, followed by a pause, will encourage additional response.
2. Restate in your own words what you think your interviewee has said in response to your question. Use this technique especially if the question or the response is complicated. By rewording the response, you can verify your understanding and give the interviewee the opportunity to clarify or give more details. If you do not understand, say so and request an explanation.
3. Ask for specific examples, definitions, illustrations, statistics, and anecdotes. These details will significantly aid your own understanding and at the same time provide excellent support for your paper.

Step 7: Take careful notes. Bring at least two pens and plenty of note paper. For key responses, be prepared to write out the speaker's exact phrases. Be sure to make notes of specifics, like names, dates, numbers, etc. In the margin of your notes, indicate the number of the question to help you locate specific responses later.

If the interviewee agrees and you have the proper equipment, you might want to tape-record the interview. If you use a tape recorder, start it and forget it. Every time you glance at it, your interviewee will do the same. Avoid the distraction. Furthermore, never rely entirely on the recorder. Mechanical things tend to malfunction when you most need them. Take notes, too.

Step 8: Conclude in timely fashion. Be sure you take no more than the agreed-upon time. If you see that you will not have a chance to ask all your questions, indicate that in the interest of time you will skip ahead in order to get to certain important matters. When your time is up, extend your thanks and leave.

Following the Interview

Step 9: Send a letter of appreciation. Your letter should thank the interviewee for both time and information. Depending on the person and his or her apparent interest in your topic, you may offer to send a copy of the completed paper. Most people find pleasure in seeing their names in print in a formal research paper.

Use details from the interview to support your thesis. Study the model papers in Chapter 14 to see how Sarah and Terry incorporated interview material in their papers.

SURVEYS

A survey is used to get information from anonymous people. Surveys can provide information about an almost unlimited range of topics: readers' preferences, insurance rates, recycling, recreation, nutrition, children's television viewing habits, home heating sources, and so on. The surveys can be as simple as a show of hands or as complicated as a multiple-page form. Either exteme may be helpful to you as primary research, but the realities of time and expense play a large part in what kind of survey you can conduct.

Preparing for a Survey

Step 1: Determine the purpose of your survey. Your purpose and topic determine what kind of survey you should use, if any. Must you provide proof of public opinion? Are you seeking support for a persuasive piece? Do you need to show opposition? Are you attempting to prove apathy? Will a local survey meet your purpose?

Step 2: Design your survey questions to meet your paper's purpose. The most difficult part of wording survey questions is to make them objective. Compare these questions:

1. Do you agree that physically handicapped citizens are given adequate opportunities for employment?

   Yes   No

2. Are physically handicapped citizens given adequate opportunities for employment?

   Yes   No

3. Are physically handicapped citizens given equal opportunities for employment?

   Yes   No

4. Physically handicapped citizens are given adequate opportunities for employment.

   Circle one number:

   strongly agree   1 2 3 4 5 6   *strongly disagree*

   Each of these questions and the response choices provided will evoke a slightly different attitude in the reader. Make sure your survey questions are impartial and unbiased.

   If you need to identify the respondents in any way, decide whether you need to know their age, sex, level of education, professional identification, political affiliation, and so on. Remember, however, that if you ask questions that are too personal, even on an anonymous survey, you may not get complete responses. Since an incomplete survey is invalid, it is worthless to your research.

   Word your questions so that they can be answered with simple responses. Only two kinds of simple answers can be tabulated:

1. a choice (like yes/no, agree/disagree, or good/bad)
2. a range response

A range response allows respondents to express a degree of choice as in question 4 in the sample series. When using a range response, always use an even number of possible choices in a range: four, six, or eight choices. This technique prevents people from giving consistently "average" answers, such as choosing response 3 in a five-item range.

Whichever response form you choose, keep the survey short and simple. Getting people to respond to a survey is hard enough without making the form complicated. Consider the following example.

As part of his paper on advertising, Ricardo is trying to determine if money-off coupons influence consumers to buy certain products. As a result, he obtained permission from a local grocer to ask shoppers who cashed in coupons to complete this five-question survey:

Dear Consumer:

Please answer these five questions as they describe your grocery shopping TODAY. Circle the most accurate response.

1. How many coupons did you cash in today?
   a. 1–3 coupons   c. 7–9 coupons
   b. 4–6 coupons   d. 10 or more coupons

2. How does the number of coupons cashed in today compare with the number you usually cash in?
   a. fewer than I usually cash in
   b. about the same as I usually cash in
   c. more than I usually cash in

3. Did you purchase any new products today as a result of money-off coupons?
   a. yes
   b. no

4. Have you ever purchased a new product as a result of a money-off coupon?
   a. yes   b. no   c. don't remember

5. Does a money-off coupon cause you to switch brands?
   a. never   c. usually
   b. sometimes   d. always

Thank you for taking time to help with my research!

Christina's research topic questions whether or not educational level influences the kind of music a person prefers. As a result, she developed a two-question survey, which she obtained permission to distribute at a local shopping mall on Saturday and Sunday afternoons. Her survey was short and sweet:

Dear Local Resident,

Please answer these two questions by circling the most accurate response.

   1. What is your *highest* level of education?
      a. elementary school
      b. high school
      c. some college
      d. college graduate
      e. postgraduate work
      f. postgraduate degree

   2. To which local radio station do you prefer to listen?
      a. WKMO (hard rock)
      b. WLOW (country-western)
      c. WNIN (public radio/classical)
      d. WROK (50s and 60s/light rock)
      e. WXTO (easy listening)

Thank you for your help with my research project.

TECH TIP

Depending on available hardware and software capabilities, you may be able to design a survey that can be tabulated on the computer. If not, consider at least the design of the survey on a word processor. Then if you find some flaw in your survey, you can quickly redo it.

Step 3: Plan a survey site. Where can you best get responses to meet the purpose of your survey? Should you knock on doors in your neighborhood, turn to your classmates, call on area churches and youth groups, or approach government offices? To get a good cross section of the population, you may want to conduct your survey at a local mall or shopping center; but be sure to check first with the management. Some businesses have policies preventing such activity.

Conducting the Survey

Step 4: Ask with a smile and a brief explanation. A friendly explanation that you are working on a school research paper will usually get a kindly response from people. Expect a few grouchy ones, but just smile, apologize, and move on. Have plenty of pencils handy. Clipboards may help, too.

Step 5: Provide a box for completed surveys, and thank people. Some people are unwilling to express an opinion to strangers. Others are unwilling to express an opinion if they can be identified. Keep these characteristics in mind as you collect completed surveys. Always thank people whether or not they complete your survey.

Use the survey results to support your thesis. The results may be summarized in tables included either in the text (see the wetlands model paper) or in an appendix. (See Chapter 15 for a model.)

EXPERIMENTS

Experiments almost always have a scientific basis, but they can address a wide range of topics. An experiment can be designed to determine the effects of pesticides on the water in a given stream, show people's reaction to a literary concept, indicate an appreciation of one dance form as compared to another, clarify response to a social issue, or even measure the effects of new legislation. Whatever the purpose, the steps of preparing for and conducting an experiment are basically the same.

Preparing the Experiment

Step 1: Raise the question. The purpose of your paper will determine your question. If, for instance, you want to find out whether the color of a plastic-worm fishing lure helps determine its effectiveness, you have raised the following question: Are fish capable of color perception?

Step 2: Collect information. You are probably already collecting information as you read your secondary resources. You will need to find out how many colors are used in plastic fishing lures, which colors professional fishermen use, which colors seem to have proven most successful, whether anyone else has done any research on this subject, and what the research shows or does not show.

Step 3: *Develop the hypothesis and determine how to prove or disprove it.* A hypothesis is an educated guess based on the information currently available. You word it as a positive statement asserting what your experiment will prove: Fish can detect colors.

CRITICAL THINKING HINT

Logic and creativity should determine the procedure by which you prove or disprove your hypothesis. The procedure may involve single or multiple steps, but it must be based on previous scientific knowledge and a logical application of fact. Above all, the test must be valid.

You might test the hypothesis that fish can detect colors by dangling six or eight different colored plastic fishing worms and noting how many fish nudge or nibble how many times at each color. You change the arrangement of the colors to prove that the fish are attracted to a worm's color, not to its position. You might have a control group and an experimental group, one well-fed and the other not, to determine whether fish react more readily to a particular color simply because they are hungry.

Conducting the Experiment

Step 4: *Tabulate and analyze the data.* As you conduct the experiment, carrying out the plan developed in Step 3, you will collect the data. In the fishing lure experiment, for instance, you will keep track of the control and experimental groups, noting how many times each color lure was nudged or nibbled when placed in each position. Your records will include dates, times, and procedures. Then you analyze what your data may show.

Step 5: *Reach a conclusion.* Based on the investigation and the tabulation and analysis of the resulting data, you will be able to reach a conclusion. The conclusion is based on data interpretation, and it will prove the hypothesis, disprove it, or prove it with certain reservations. Report the experiment, its procedures and conclusion, as part of the support for your thesis.

LETTERS

Requesting information by letter may sometimes be the only practical or economical means by which you can obtain a personal response from an authority in a given field. In addition, response to a letter can add a creative touch to an otherwise tired topic. For instance, Shawn is writing his paper on capital punishment, a tired, old topic for high school research papers. To add life to his work, however, he has added a significant dimension with primary research by writing to a prison warden, a judge, and prisoner on death row. In each case, he has asked questions whose answers will help develop his working outline.

Patty is writing her paper on the effects of alcohol abuse, another tired, old topic for high school research papers. By seeking a variety of primary resources, however, she has added not only a contemporary dimension to the paper, but she has given the topic a personal touch. Her letters went to a state police post investigating alcohol-related traffic deaths, a medical examiner investigating alcohol-related suicides, the Alcoholics Anonymous local chapter president, and four teenagers who are admitted alcoholics, two of whom are undergoing treatment. Their combined responses to Patty's questions will give firsthand insight into the multiple effects of alcohol abuse.

Follow these guidelines for letters seeking primary research:

Step 1: *Write courteous letters explaining your purpose.* By clarifying that you are writing a research paper, you put the reader in the position of an authority who can help you solve a problem or understand an issue. Making your reader feel important will help him or her feel more comfortable responding to a stranger's letter about what may be a personal matter.

Step 2: *Request specific information.* Without specific questions, your reader may respond with all kinds of interesting material but nothing that will serve your purpose or support your working outline. Ask questions similar to those for an interview: open-ended questions that cannot be answered by *yes* or *no* and that come from your working outline.

Step 3: *Make the response easy.* You can make the response easy in several ways. First, you can leave space in your letter after each question for the reader to respond. In that manner, a reply does not require a fully composed letter. You give your reader a quick out. Second, provide a stamped self-addressed envelope. Third, if you think your reader may not feel comfortable writing a response, suggest that, if preferable, you will send a blank tape for recorded remarks.

In dealing with highly personal topics, readers may prefer to remain anonymous. Make that offer in your letter. Some readers will respond more readily if they feel assured their names will not be used. Cite such references either under an assumed name or listed in the bibliography as "anonymous."

Step 4: Allow ample response time. Always indicate when you want the letter returned, but give your reader ample response time. Your letter may take several days or even a week to reach its destination. Busy people prioritize their response to mail, and yours may not be on top. Give readers at least three weeks to respond. The postal service will add several days to that date.

Step 5: Accept the fact that some people will not respond. Certainly, you cannot force someone to respond to your letter. Your courtesy can encourage the response, but sometimes your best efforts will be futile. In any case, do not beg.

Step 6: Thank those who respond. Courtesy demands that you thank anyone who responds. The thanks can be in the form of a letter or some other token appropriate to the situation and the person.

Some respondents may enjoy reading your final paper. If so, be sure to send them courtesy copies as part of your appreciation for their contribution.

TECH TIP

While e-mail is fast, convenient, and cheap (no paper, envelopes, or stamps required), common courtesy still calls for a handwritten thank-you note to anyone who helps you with your primary research. And sooner is better than later for your courtesy note.

TIME MANAGEMENT GUIDELINES

Although you will no doubt conduct your primary research simultaneously with your secondary research reading and note taking, allow a few days for the preparation and compilation of materials. The following guidelines should help you allocate time:

Number of weeks to work on final paper	Number of days available for seeking primary resources
10	5
8	4
6	2
4	1

Two Students' Progress

Both Sarah and Terry incorporated primary resources in their papers. Each had a different experience regarding the interview. For Sarah, the interview provided added information or clarification about issues she had already read about. For Terry, the interview provided the catalyst for developing his final thesis. But let them tell their own stories.

Sarah

By the time I had read some of my secondary resources, I knew I wanted to be able to explain why wetlands are important to everyone, even to folks in big cities. While my sources gave all kinds of statistics and information about the loss of wetlands and their importance, I needed some personal reaction from a live human being.

My dad's fishing buddy told me that the Division of Fish and Wildlife probably had someone on staff who could talk about wetlands. I called the headquarters of a local wildlife area, got the man's name, and called for an appointment. He was great! Not only did he seem happy to talk about his favorite topic, but he hunted up some brochures for me.

But I'm ahead of myself. When I called for the appointment, the biologist wanted to know what questions I had, and I was prepared to tell him I'd be sending a list of questions. The interview was scheduled for two weeks later, so I e-mailed the questions the next day. That gave him plenty of time to think about what I needed before the interview date. Here's the e-mail I sent:

Dear Mr. Poole:

Thank you for agreeing to an interview with me about the wetlands issue. I'm looking forward to hearing your point of view.

I'd especially like to hear your opinions on the following four questions:

1. Hunters, fishermen, and bird-watchers have a personal interest in wetlands, but what can we say to other folks to help them gain a personal interest in wetlands as well? How can we make them feel wetlands are important to them personally?

2. The literature I've read suggests that farmers are the biggest enemy to wetlands, yet I have read about one farmer who believes "wetlands have a kind of net positive value to agriculture." In your view, what is the net positive value of wetlands on agriculture?

3. Greed seems to be the underlying factor when wetlands are destroyed. How can we attach a dollar value to wetlands to gain public support from folks who see no problem draining a wetland area in order to build new industry and provide more jobs? How do we combat the "dollars and sense war"?

4. Many people don't really understand the term "wetlands" or that it can apply to a wide variety of areas (marshes, bogs, swamps, estuaries, coastal areas, river and stream banks) and that wetlands can be a quarter acre or hundreds of acres. In light of that fact, what do you think needs to happen in order to save the precious few remaining wetlands?

I'm looking forward to the opportunity to talk with you for about 45 minutes in your office at 3:30 on Thursday, April 18. With your permission, I will plan to tape the interview so that I can include accurate quotations in my paper.

My sincere thanks for your willingness to clear your schedule to see me at that time.

Sincerely,

Sarah Blaser

The interview lasted almost an hour because Mr. Poole said he had the few minutes' extra time and was interested in addressing all my questions. I took notes during the interview and also recorded Mr. Poole's comments. The tape ran out after thirty minutes and I forgot to turn it over, so I was glad I had my notes. As it turned out, I never did play back the tape; my notes were adequate and quicker to use than finding specific spots on the tape.

After the interview, I sent a thank-you letter:

April 20, ____

Mr. Keith Poole
Wetlands Biologist
Division of Fish and Wildlife
Department of Natural Resources
R.R. 6, Box 344
Peru, IN 46970

Dear Mr. Poole:

Thank you for taking time to talk with me last Thursday. Your expertise and insights will, without a doubt, enhance my research paper. I appreciate the preparation you did in order to respond to my questions, as well as your candid remarks about a matter that means a great deal to both of us.

Best wishes for your continued success in a career you so obviously enjoy.

Sincerely,

Sarah
Sarah Blaser

Terry

My assignment required the use of two primary sources: the Steinbeck novel and an interview. We were to interview someone who lived during the Great Depression. I decided to interview my grandfather. Even though he lives about two hours' drive from home, I didn't call ahead. After all, the family was going for a visit that weekend, so I knew he'd be around whenever we found time to talk.

I had finished reading *The Grapes of Wrath* before our visit. In fact, I had a list of questions related to my key points: religion and family unity. Mostly, though, I let Grandfather talk about the family problems as he remembered them. Occasionally he mentioned a topic that seemed to parallel what I'd read in *The Grapes of Wrath*, so I'd ask a few lead questions. For instance, he talked about how the family never missed a church service. That caused me to recall the role of religion in *The Grapes of Wrath*, so I asked for more details.

The interview turned out to be the catalyst that helped me organize my paper and decide precisely what my thesis would be.

TIPS AND TRAPS

While using primary resources can enhance a paper, be prepared for possible pitfalls. "You'd be surprised how much time it takes to do primary research. I was amazed that I spent all evening just setting up an interview and writing the follow-up letter," Sarah warned. "And some of my friends did surveys; one did an experiment. It seemed to me they were always talking about what they still had to do to pull it all together."

Terry countered, "Maybe they talked about that part of their research because it was the most interesting. It's sure a lot more fun to actually *do* something than to just read and read and read some more. I really enjoyed doing the interview for my paper, and I think most of the class felt the same way."

Terry's comment suggests, however, something else to look out for: be sure that you do not neglect the secondary references in favor of the primary research. A good balance is essential.

CHECKLIST FOR USING PRIMARY RESOURCES

You should be able to answer an honest "yes" to each of the following questions.

1. Considering my purpose and narrowed topic, have I considered the most likely possibilities for primary resources?
2. Have I read my secondary references widely enough to know which primary sources will be of benefit and how they can enhance my research paper?
3. Have I made an honest effort to seek available community resources?
4. After locating a potential source for an interview, did I follow logical steps for the interview process?
   a. Did I arrange for an appointment?
   b. Did I prepare a list of questions to address my purpose and my specific topic?

    c. Did I write a letter or an e-mail of confirmation and include a list of questions for the interview?

    d. Did I prioritize the questions?

    e. Did I conduct the interview in a timely, gracious fashion?

    f. Did I listen critically to the interviewee's responses and ask logical follow-up questions?

    g. Did I express appreciation both at the conclusion of the interview and in a follow-up letter?

5. If my purpose and topic suggested the need for it, did I plan and conduct a successful survey?

    a. Did I include questions seeking information directly related to my purpose and topic?

    b. Did I word the questions objectively?

    c. If necessary, did I provide for a way to identify the source of responses?

    d. Did I conduct the survey in a timely, gracious fashion?

    e. Did I tabulate the results fairly?

6. If my purpose and topic suggested the need for it, did I plan and conduct a successful experiment?

    a. Did I develop a clear hypothesis?

    b. Did I design testing procedures that would prove or disprove the hypothesis?

    c. Did I gather accurate data and analyze it impartially?

    d. Did I reach a logical conclusion based on the data?

7. If my purpose and topic suggested it, did I write effective letters to potential sources?

    a. Did I ask for specific information relevant to my research question?

    b. Did I allow ample response time?

    c. Did I express my appreciation to those who responded?

8. Have I managed my time well?

EXERCISES

Exercise A: *Evaluating Interview Questions*

Directions: Using Sarah's e-mail on pages 119–120, discuss the following questions.

1. In each of the four questions, Sarah begins with a statement. What is the purpose of the statement?

2. Should all interview questions included in a letter of confirmation be written in this way? Why or why not?

3. Questions 1 and 3 actually each contain two questions. Why do you think Sarah puts them together as if they were one?

4. Which questions ask for personal opinions? Is that valid research?

5. Do the questions appear to be in any order? Will it matter which one Sarah asks first? Why or why not?

6. Sarah lists only four questions for her planned 45-minute interview. Does that seem like a reasonable number of questions for the time? Why or why not?

Exercise B: Evaluating Survey Questions

Directions: On page 112 you will find four survey questions. Refer to them for the following questions.

1. How does the word "agree" influence the reader in question 1?

2. How does the word "adequate" influence the reader in question 2 of the survey?

3. How does the word "equal" influence the reader in question 3?

4. How does the range of responses from "strongly agree" to "strongly disagree" influence the reader in question 4?

5. If you were designing a survey on a similar topic, which, of any, of these four questions would you use? Why?

Exercise C: Evaluating the Experimental Procedure

Directions: As part of his research on manufacturers' recommended mainte-nance procedures for a new car, Gene plans to test five major brands of car wax. Decide whether there are any flaws in the following steps of his planned experiment. You will find responses to the first three to serve as a model.

1. He will use a trunk lid from a recent model car that had been de-molished in an accident.
Model Response: Valid. By using a single component from one car, Gene guarantees he is testing the different waxes on the same paint of the same age with the same wear.

2. The trunk lid is slightly bowed from the impact, but otherwise the paint is unharmed.
Model Response: Bowing, not various waxes, could cause the paint to peel off. If paint remains in place, the test spots should otherwise be valid.

3. He will purchase five major brands of car wax.

Model Response: Valid. By choosing only five major brands, Gene will have ample space on the trunk lid to apply and test all five.

4. He will paint lines horizontally across the trunk lid to separate the surface into five areas.

5. He will clean the entire trunk lid with a strong detergent and water.

6. In each of the five areas he will apply wax according to the manufacturers' directions.

7. He will determine if one wax immediately produces a glossier finish than another.

8. He will leave the trunk lid in full sun so that all areas are equally affected.

9. After a week, he will determine if one wax remains glossier than another.

10. He will now wash the entire trunk lid with mild soap and water every day, rinsing with water, leaving the lid in full sun.

11. After a week, he will again determine if one wax remains glossier than another.

12. His findings will determine whether one wax is superior to another in protecting paint surfaces.

Exercise D: Writing the Right Letters

Directions: List at least two sources to whom a researcher could write letters seeking primary information for the following topics.

1. environmental impact of oil spills

2. importance of reading aloud to preschool children

3. value of planting and protecting urban trees

4. comparison of various auto insurance plans

5. effects of climate change on streets and roads

6. comparison of Clinton's and Bush's first presidential campaigns

7. role of ethnic leadership in local government

8. how state budgets are made

9. how the Indianapolis 500 affects the development of standard automobiles

10. impact of the laser on the average person

11. analysis of Thomas Hardy's *The Return of the Native*

12. comparison of two newspapers' treatment of a school issue

Exercise E: *Writing Your Own Letter*

Directions: Using the guidelines in Chapter 6, write a letter to a primary resource seeking information that will support the development of your working outline. Use good form.

7

Taking Notes

Taking notes will require the largest block of time in the research process. Your notes determine your paper—its contents, its emphasis, its accuracy, its success. Good notes, therefore, are essential to a good paper. This chapter will provide guidelines for good note taking and offer realistic suggestions for ensuring their quality and accuracy. To more thoroughly understand the importance of good note taking, you may wish to study Chapters 7 and 8 together. Chapter 8 shows how notes become the text of the paper. It helps you see not only why but how notes become the backbone of your finished paper.

GENERAL GUIDELINES

As you take notes from any source, follow these general guidelines:

1 *Before you take notes, number your bibliography cards.* The numbering serves two purposes: First, it speeds note taking by allowing you to cite just the number of the bibliography card rather than a full title or author name on the note card. Second, it speeds the documentation of your paper's first draft by allowing you to cite only a pair of numbers rather than a full name and page reference. Although the order in which you number does not matter, it is a good idea to use numbers to help identify the kinds of sources. Thus, you may choose to number book references beginning with 1, magazine or other periodical references beginning with 25, and electronic references beginning with 50. To make the numbers obvious on the bibliography cards, write them in a contrasting color, perhaps red. (Note that this numbering is unrelated to the order you will use for the Works Cited page.)

2 *Take notes on index cards of a distinct size or color.* Use either 3″ × 5″ or 4″ × 6″ cards for your notes. It is a good idea to use a different size or a different color for note cards than for bibliography cards. If, however, you use the larger cards for notes, do not be tempted to fill them completely.

TECH TIP

Some computer supply stores stock note-card-size printer paper. You can use it by adjusting the page length setting or by using the return key to begin printing a new note.

If you are unable to find the special printer paper, you can still space notes so that a standard 8½″ × 11″ paper will accommodate three or four notes. Use the line guide on your screen to determine spacing. For purposes of sorting and organizing later, cut the page into strips after it leaves the printer.

3 *Put only one idea from one source on a note card.* Even though you may have only a few words on a card, do not put more than one idea from one source on a card. Later you will organize the note cards according to your outline. Thus, if you put more than one idea on a card, you will face an impossible task when you try to organize them.

4 *Use ink.* If you do not use word processing to prepare your notes, use ink for handwritten notes. Pencil smears, and after you handle the cards, the penciled notes may become difficult to read.

5 *Write on only one side of the card.* If you write on the reverse side, you may forget to look there later. If you absolutely cannot complete a note on one side of one card (as in a long quotation, for instance), write "continued" or "more" on the first card to remind you to look for the second.

6 *Identify the source.* On every note card identify the number of the source from which the note comes. The source, of course, gets its number from the bibliography card. (See step 1, page 127.) Write that same source number in the upper right corner of every note card taken from that source, and circle the source number to distinguish it from the page number(s). The source identification is essential since every fact or opinion included in your paper must be documented, whether it is quoted or stated in your own words.

7 *Identify the page number.* On every note card identify the page number or, in the case of a Web page without a page number, the paragraph number from which the note comes. Write it in the upper right corner after the source number. To forget to record the page or paragraph number now will mean searching through hundreds of resources later, seeking the spot in which you found a specific bit of information. For best results, establish a routine for taking notes. Make it part of your routine to list source and page or paragraph numbers *first*. Then take notes. Since the discovery of a missing page reference or missing source number usually comes late at night when libraries are closed, you will save yourself much agony by paying careful attention now.

TECH TIP

Web sites typically do not have page numbers. Instead, the pages will be designated by an extension of the basic URL address. For instance, a URL like www.audubon.org may have a Web page somewhere in the site whose URL is www.audubon.org/maps/states. If you retrieve information from that page, you must record that page in your Works Cited page. So make sure that when you take notes from a Web site, you record of the exact URL of that respective page.

8 *Identify the topic.* On every note card identify the topic by a word or two. These identifying words are called the *slug* and should come from your outline. Adding a slug now will keep you from having to reread the entire note card later to decide where it fits in the paper. Do *not* use outline numbers (like III B or IV A) because you will probably change your outline as you work. Using slugs—like Sarah's "Definition," "Farmer's destruction," and "Urban wetlands"—will allow you to change the outline without losing the identification of your note cards. (See Chapter 2, pages 32–33, for sample working outlines and Chapter 9, pages 168–169, for complete outlines.)

CRITICAL THINKING HINT

Your outline guides your note taking. If you are about to take a note for which there is no logical slug from your outline, you have one of two problems:

1. Your outline needs revision in order to include this new idea. Revise and use the new slug.
   OR
2. The note, while interesting, is irrelevant to your topic. Avoid taking notes that will not support your thesis.

9 *Strive for representation from many sources.* It stands to reason that some sources will simply be more valuable than others. Be sure, however, that you do not rely too heavily on only one or two sources, even if one of these sources is the World Wide Web. To do so is to show a lack of proficiency in the research process. If you have twenty note cards from one book or one Web source, for example, five from another, and only one or two from each of your other sources, you have relied too heavily on a single source.

10 *Do not number note cards.* You will sort and organize them later when you are ready to write your first draft. To number them now is wasted effort.

11 *Check graphics.* Do not overlook information in charts, tables, photographs, diagrams, maps, or other illustrations that may help support your thesis. You may even choose to redraw or make a photocopy of a particularly helpful table or figure to include in your own paper, with proper documentation, of course.

12 *Take adequate notes.* It is better to have too many notes than too few. If several notes duplicate an idea, you can later choose the best or use the duplicates to prove that several authorities agree.

13 *Double-check every note card.* Before you leave a note card and go on to the next, check to see that four kinds of information are included: source number, page or paragraph number(s), slug, and note. Use abbreviations, symbols, or signs to help speed you through the note-taking process. Just be sure you can remember what the abbreviations mean!

14 *Let your outline guide your reading.* Always remember that your outline maps out your work. Otherwise, you will waste valuable time reading or taking notes on irrelevant material.

15 *Think before you write.* Before you take a note, ask yourself three questions:

- How will this information help me support my thesis statement?
- What is this material really saying?
- How can I use this in my paper?

Do not spend more time copying than thinking.

16 *Add notes to yourself.* As you gather information on your note cards, you may want to make parenthetical notes to yourself about the contents. For example, you may add "contradicts Pearcy," "may need more detail here," or "use for final argument?"

TECH TIP

You can take notes at the keyboard, but avoid doing so unless the equipment will be available for the entire project. Here are some suggestions:

Format text with margins to resemble 3″ × 5″ or 4″ × 6″ note cards. This format will help you avoid taking notes that are too lengthy. Enter the slug, source code, page or paragraph number, and note as you would for a handwritten note card, and save all the notes from that source in one file.

Next, create new files by slug. Use copy and paste (not cut and paste) to move all notes with the same slug into one file. By using copy instead of cut, you avoid the risk of losing text as you move it from one file to another. Also, by maintaining files by source, you avoid the risk of losing track of which text came from where. And by creating a file for each slug, you reduce the effort involved in preparing your first draft.

Finally, always generate a print copy and a backup file when you finish each set of source notes. Better to have extra copies than none at all when something (almost inevitably) goes awry with the technology.

17 *Handle photocopied materials carefully.* If you make photocopies of any material, either because you cannot check it out of the library or because you intend to use it in your paper, be sure also to photocopy the title and copyright pages for documentation purposes. Be sure, too, that you do not cut off the page numbers when you make copies.

EVALUATING SOURCES

As you begin reading to take notes, you need to judge the value of your sources. Good sources can suggest ways to organize your material or limit your topic, and they can give you supporting details or refutation. You learned in Chapter 4 how to evaluate Web sites, so consider now the following four criteria for judging books, magazines, and other periodicals:

1 *Relevance* No one expects you to read entire books about your research topic, so you must decide if this source really addresses your topic. Check the table of contents for key chapters. Read the introduction or preface for clues about the book's intent or the author's purpose. Check the index for appropriate headings and cross references. Look through the appendix and the glossary. Is there valuable information?

2 *Timeliness* If your topic deals with a contemporary issue, old sources probably have little credibility except for historical perspective. Generally, the more current a source, the better. On the other hand, if your topic addresses historical events, you can expect to find few recent sources unless they analyze the events in light of recent circumstances. Often, however, a standard reference is revised periodically. Seek the most recent edition, since it is usually the most reliable.

3 *Authorship* When you find a name appearing in multiple bibliographies or when you find multiple articles by the same author, you can reasonably assume that he or she maintains some credibility, especially if published in reliable sources. What is a reliable source? That depends on the topic. Brad will not find suitable information about the geology of mud slides in *Good Housekeeping* but he might in *Scientific American*.

4 *Slant* Different sources will approach a topic differently, depending on the intended audience. For example, *Newsweek* will take a different editorial slant about the urban crime rate than does *The New York Times*.

Local newspapers, some more objective than others, tend to treat national news in terms of its effect on local interests. A general encyclopedia like *World Book* takes a different approach to its coverage of the Korean conflict than does the *Encyclopedia of American History.* Likewise, *Family Circle* will address the issue of school choice differently than does the *NEA Journal* (National Education Association). As a rule of thumb, journals are more reliable than magazines because magazines will tailor articles to their readership, perhaps printing only one side of an issue. On the other hand, journals will be more technical and less easily understood by lay readers.

The publishing house will also have some bearing on the material's slant. For instance, if a special interest group publishes material, you can be certain the material supports that group's cause. Be wary, for instance, of a book about acid rain published by a coal company.

In short, be alert to editorial slant. The best precaution is to select a wide range of resources.

AVOIDING PLAGIARISM

Plagiarism is literary theft. It is using someone else's words or ideas—whether from a print source or off the Internet—as if they were your own. Because it is considered such a serious offense, most colleges and universities have policies severely penalizing students who plagiarize. Some policies call for automatic failure in the class involved, and some even call for expulsion. With such severe ramifications possible, it is best to learn from the outset how to avoid the offense.

Study the following four passages. The first is the original passage by Aurelia Kamp. The second passage illustrates plagiarism. The third passage accurately rewords, quotes, and documents the words and ideas used from the original. The fourth passage accurately rewords and documents the ideas from the original but does not include direct quotes.

Original Passage

The cost-effective production of white corn is important to anyone who likes cereal for breakfast, tacos for lunch, tortillas for dinner, or fritos for a snack. But reducing operating costs in order to keep down consumer costs is an ongoing problem for farmers. As we walked through the grain-bin area, Mr. Z. pointed to a 3,500-gallon propane tank. During harvest, he explained, the tank was filled every other day. Then, to reduce costs, Mr. Z. spent $70,000 to design and build a cob burner that gasifies the corncobs and turns them into fuel. The operation has cut the fuel bill by 60%. Now the propane fuel tank is filled only once a week.

Plagiarized (Not Acceptable)

Reducing the operating costs of white corn production is an ongoing problem, but one farmer has reduced costs by spending $70,000 to design and build a cob burner that gasifies the corncobs and turns them into fuel.

Notice that although the order of the passage has been altered and that a few of the words have been omitted, the passage is basically the same as the original. No quotation marks set off the exact words of the original and no documentation acknowledges the source. *Both* must occur in order to avoid plagiarism. Compare that with the following:

Reworded, Partly Quoted, and Documented (Acceptable)

Farmers struggle to reduce the cost of producing white corn, a staple for many Americans who like cereal and tortillas. One farmer has cut his fuel consumption in half by using what had once been thrown away: the corncobs. As Mr. Z. explained, the $70,000 cob burner "gasifies the corncobs and turns them into fuel" (Kamp 16).

In this acceptably written passage, exact words appear in quotation marks and the reworded portions are acknowledged by documentation at the end of the paragraph. Notice in the following passage, however, that no exact phrases appear.

Reworded and Documented (Acceptable)

Representative of farmers' creative approaches to cut the cost of producing white corn, one farmer has given the term "recycling" a new twist. For $70,000 he designed and built a cob burner that turns corncobs to gas that can in turn be used for fuel. He has eliminated the pile of cobs that accumulated out back and at the same time cut his fuel consumption by more than half (Kamp 16).

Completely reworded, this passage omits exact words from the source; thus, no quotation marks are necessary to mark them. Since the passage is a summary, however, credit must be given to the source.

Let's put all this in simple form. To avoid plagiarism, you must adhere to three rules:

1. *DO NOT* use exact words from a source without putting them inside quotation marks and giving credit to the source.
2. *DO NOT* reword a passage without giving credit to the source.
3. *DO NOT* summarize a passage without giving credit to the source.

In other words, be honest about where you get your words and ideas and you will never be guilty of theft. Of course, your own ideas and interpretations need no source identification.

KINDS OF NOTES

As you take notes for your paper, you will find different kinds of notes necessary in different situations. Most writers use the following six kinds of notes: direct quotation, partial quotation, précis, outline, paraphrase, and combination.

Direct Quotation

A note for a direct quotation changes nothing from the source. Spelling, punctuation, words—everything must be on the note card exactly as it appears in the source. (If a word is misspelled or incorrectly used, add the word *sic* in brackets, meaning "thus," to clarify that the error is not yours.) Remember to use quotation marks around exact words. You will be guilty of plagiarism if you forget!

Use direct quotations sparingly in your note cards for two main reasons:

1. Too many quotations will make your paper choppy. Since no two writers write in the same style, any quotations in your paper will be in a style unlike your own. In fact, less than 20% of your final paper should be quoted material. Save time later by putting information on the note cards in your own words.
2. Copying quotations and checking their accuracy takes longer than writing in your own words a summary, a few key phrases, or main ideas.

The obvious question, of course, is when do you use direct quotations? Use direct quotations

- when an authority's words carry weight (especially in a persuasive paper, in an opinion paper, or in a controversial issue)
- when the quotation is concise (so a summary or paraphrase causes the words to lose their impact)
- when it would be impossible to restate as effectively in your own words

The following illustrates a quotation note:

Direct Quotation Note

Destruction (16) 45

"Thanks to a double-dealing U.S.D.A.,
Swampbuster's a bust, wetlands are
being destroyed, and taxpayers are
getting soaked for it."

Note that if your quotation, in turn, includes another quotation, you must enclose the included quote in single quotation marks. Your note will be punctuated as follows: "The ultimate decision for apologizing is, according to D. Collins, 'up to the offending party.'"

Partial Quotation

Frequently, a note card will be only a partial quotation. In other words, for the most part you will summarize or write in your own words, quoting only some key phrase. Such notes follow a few simple rules:

1. Use the ellipsis (a series of three periods separated by a space between each, like this . . .) to represent the omission of a word or words. If the omission occurs at the end of a sentence, a fourth period serves as the end mark, like this. . . . Remember to use quotation marks around the quoted material!

2. Use brackets [like this] to insert your own words inside a quotation or to change a word form (for example, from *usual* to *usual*[*ly*]). Do not use parentheses instead. Again, remember to use quotation marks around the quoted material.

The following changes may be made without using brackets:

3. changing a verb tense (in order to maintain consistent tense in your own paper)

4. changing uppercase letters to lowercase or lowercase to uppercase to suit your sentence structure
5. omitting or altering the final punctuation mark to suit your own sentence structure

The following note card illustrates a partial quotation.

Partial Quotation Note

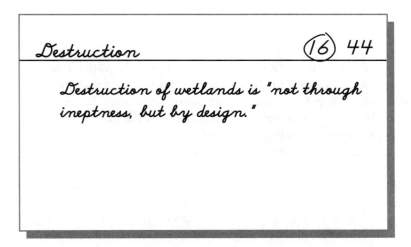

Destruction   (16) 44

Destruction of wetlands is "not through ineptness, but by design."

Précis

A note card that summarizes is a précis. Usually a précis is about one-third the length of the original. To be accurate, a précis must maintain the same tone and the same message as the original.

CRITICAL THINKING HINT

Since a précis must maintain the same tone and the same message as the original, you must think analytically. Ask yourself key questions about the original passage and your précis:

- What is the author's message?
- How does he or she feel about the subject?
- How do this author's feelings differ from those of others I have read?

- If the author could talk to me personally, in what tone of voice would he or she express these ideas?
- Have I expressed the same idea in the same tone of voice on my note card?

Read the following passage and compare it with the sample précis that follows it.

Original Passage

The food habits of birds make them especially valuable to agriculture. Because birds have higher body temperatures, more rapid digestion, and greater energy than most other animals, they require more food. Nestling birds grow very rapidly, requiring huge amounts of food. They usually consume as much as or more than their own weight in soft-bodied insects every day.

For instance, robins have been observed to gain eight times their original weight the first eight days of their lives. Insect-eating birds must fill their stomachs five to six times daily because they digest their food so fast and because of the large amount of indigestible material in insects. One young robin, weighing three ounces, consumed 165 cutworms weighing 5½ ounces in one day. If a ten-pound baby ate at the same rate, he or she would eat 18⅓ pounds of food in a day.

Of course, birds cannot control insects completely, but they are of great value. By using soil- and water-conserving practices, farmers and ranchers could probably double the population of helpful birds. Field and farmstead windbreaks, living fences, shrub buffers, grass waterways, and farm ponds are only a few of the many land use practices useful in attracting and increasing beneficial forms of wildlife.

Précis

A bird's metabolism causes it to eat relatively more than most other animals. In addition, since insects aren't fully digestible, insect-eating birds may fill their stomachs five or six times a day. We can double the numbers of insect-eaters by attracting them with trees, shrubs, and ponds.

TECH TIP

Remember that taking notes from the Web is no different than taking notes from print sources. In fact, since you will no doubt print out what you find on the Web, in effect your notes will come from a print source after all!

Outline

An outline note may appear in formal outline style or look more like a list. In either case, it is particularly appropriate when noting a series of points or steps.

Outline Note

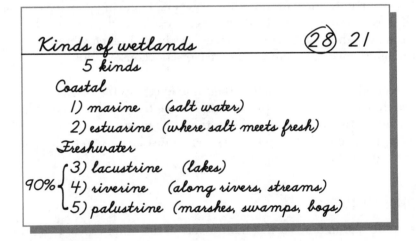

Paraphrase

The paraphrase can be fatal. Because it is a rewording of the original passage, a paraphrase is most likely to lean toward plagiarism. Nevertheless, the paraphrased note is essential when you need to simplify complicated text or when you need to clarify a passage. Be absolutely sure when you paraphrase that you do not slip in phrases from the original. Compare the following passage with its paraphrase. (Also reread the paraphrase in the section "Avoiding Plagiarism," page 133.)

Original Passage

Windows are the home's giant energy eaters. As the world grows more energy conscious, homeowners seek more ways to seal the leaks that allow heating dollars to flow freely through escape routes. They add insulation to the ceiling; they add weather stripping around doors and windows; they caulk cracks and crevices; they add storm windows or thermal panes. After all such measures have been taken, however, there seems little else to do. Wrong! About 35% of household heat can escape through windows—even those carefully caulked and protected with storm windows.

Paraphrase

Homeowners who are concerned about energy do everything they know to conserve. They add ceiling insulation, weather stripping, caulking, and storm windows, hoping to stop the exodus of heat from their winter homes and dollars from their thinning wallets. Unfortunately, most of those homeowners, believing they have done all they can to conserve heat, ignore the expanse of glass called windows. About 35% of heat loss occurs here. In fact, windows remain the worst enemy to effective energy conservation.

A good paraphrase is about the same length as the original, simplifies the language, presents the same ideas in the same order, maintains the same tone, delivers the same message, but avoids using the same phrases. Of course, you must be certain to document the source of every paraphrase.

Combination

The combination note card combines any of the other types. It is probably the most useful and the most used. Study the following combination note cards from Sarah's paper:

Farmers' destruction of wetlands (14) 19

Remove incentives to farmers to eliminate
wetlands:
1) 1986 Tax Reform Act (can't deduct)
2) 1985 Swampbuster "removes
federal flood and crop insurance
and price supports" if destroy
3) 1982 Coastal Barrier Resources Act

(1)   Combines outline and quotation

Urban wetlands (20) 32-33

4,000 acres - Portland, OR
1,232 acres - Ft. Collins, CO
13,000 acres - within Brooklyn
                and Queens
                Madison, WI
6 sq. mi. - Bellevue, WA
108 acres -

Find out:
How many acres in 6 sq. mi.

(2)   Combines list with writer's response

Laws Protecting (14) 19

Section 404 "exempts activities
connected with 'normal' farming and
forestry practices ..."

(Here is where biggest
conversions occur.)

(3)   Combines quotation and summary
      statement explaining significance of quotation

TIME MANAGEMENT GUIDELINES

Taking notes requires the largest block of time in the research process. At least three activities will take your time now.

First, of course, you will be reading and taking notes. Set aside uninterrupted time blocks of at least an hour each. Use the guides available to reduce your reading time: tables of contents, indexes, chapter headings, subheadings, and database abstracts. Skim for keywords and main ideas, and then read for details where appropriate. Take notes quickly, eliminating unneeded sentences, phrases, words. Remember that your notes need not be in complete sentences.

Second, you will also be altering your working outline as suggested by the information you turn up. You may add, delete, or only rearrange; certainly you will generate specific subtopics for your outline.

Third, you will most likely find yourself returning to the library to search for additional references. Perhaps you will not find everything you need in your first search; your sources may not prove as helpful as you thought they would be. In addition, your outline may change enough to require new information.

All this takes time—time to read, time to think about and digest what you have read, time to make accurate and complete notes, time to analyze the outline and its necessary changes, time to get to and from the library, time to make additional and perhaps more complicated searches for resources. Plan to allow plenty of time for this part of the research process, and plan to work steadily during the entire time period. Use the following guideline for your plans:

Number of weeks until final paper is due	Number of days available to complete note cards
10	10
8	8
6	6
4	4

TWO STUDENTS' PROGRESS

Busy students will tell you that taking notes demands discipline. Those who procrastinate will have to work fast and late—and inevitably will do a miserable, perhaps failing job. Sarah and Terry share their own experiences.

Sarah

Taking notes nearly put me under! I had all these books and magazines piled in my room—on the floor, on my desk, in my book bag. I found that I needed to use every spare minute to get the job done. I skipped my favorite TV shows all week and— even harder—stayed off the telephone and computer. Fortunately, most of my friends were also working on their research papers, so we understood each other's problems.

Funny things happened as I plowed through these books, magazines, and Web sources I'd printed out. I decided to start with the database stuff because it included definitions and statistics— background things. Then I looked at the magazines. I found out right away that some of the magazines I found on databases were useless. Others, though, were packed with information. When I finally started on the books, I realized that even the most current were too dated to be helpful, except for definitions and historical background.

I found myself making lots of changes in my outline. Originally (see my comments in Chapter 1) I planned to give just a simple definition of wetlands. That proved impossible, and I found myself taking several notes about the arguments over the definition. My original outline had no subtopics for the causes of destruction since I didn't know what they were. Finally, I had planned to write about the effects of wetlands destruction on plants, animals, and humans. Those headings proved illogical, not only because humans are animals but also because the list was too limiting. Then, because I found so much information on what we need to do to preserve wetlands, I added another section to my working outline. When I finished taking notes, my outline had changed to this:

I. Background of problem
   A. Rate of loss
   B. Struggle for definition
   C. Causes of destruction

II. Effects of destruction
   A. On plant life
   B. On marine life
   C. On birds
   D. On land animals
   E. On water table

III. Value to humans
    A. General purposes
    B. Dollar impact

IV. Ways to save
    A. Present regulations
    B. Future needs

(See Chapter 2, page 32, for the working outline and Chapter 9, pages 168–169, for the final outline.)

By the time I finished, I had about 70 note cards. Of those, only a couple were filled (mostly early ones before I forced myself to summarize). Some had a few words or statistics, and most were a couple of sentences. Out of the total, I had a half dozen duplicate ideas. Later I made more changes to my outline, so I ended up actually using about 50 of my notes. I guess my message is, don't be afraid to take more notes than you think you'll need. Otherwise when you start writing your paper, you may have to stop, go back to the library, and find more material.

Terry

I waited until I had completed my interview before I did my secondary research. By that time I had revised my outline and knew what I needed from library resources to support the main ideas. Since so much of my paper had to come from the novel and from the interview, many of my notes were anecdotes or responses from interview questions. I had really specific needs by the time I began surveying secondary sources.

To use my time most efficiently, I referred to the tables of contents and indexes to find details to support my three main ideas. Because my assignment was to look for a truth or insight into life as expressed in *The Grapes of Wrath*, the novel was my basic source; so I was looking for specific quotations, anecdotes, and supporting details.

From experience, I can add one bit of advice. As soon as you jot down a note, no matter what kind or how short or how long, *immediately* write down the source, including the page number. What a headache if you forget.

TIPS AND TRAPS

You can avoid the worst traps in note taking by following these two simple reminders:

1. Be sure to note the source and the page or paragraph number.
2. Do not plagiarize.

If you forget to list the source and page or paragraph number, the note card is useless because you must not use someone else's ideas without documenting the source. That takes you to the second reminder.

Some students commit plagiarism through carelessness. They simply forget to put quotation marks around exact words or forget to document the source. Carelessness, however, is no excuse. Terry found a clever way to assure himself that he did not plagiarize. "Every time I completed a note card, I used a code to note whether I quoted, summarized, or paraphrased. I used quotation marks if I quoted, wrote "sum" for summary, or wrote "pf" for paraphrase. Before I left a card, I made sure that one of those three indications appeared on the card. Later, I didn't have to guess about quotations."

Probably the most difficult task for beginning research writers is to avoid the temptation to use too many quotations. Quote a source only when he or she has said something so profound or with such authority that changing the words ruins the message. As Sarah explains, she had trouble with this concept: "We were warned early not to take many quotation notes, but that was really hard because everything I read sounded just right. I mean, these folks are professional writers, so how could I say it any better? It seemed easier just to copy down exact words and put in the quotation marks. That practice got me in trouble. We had to show the first 15 note cards to our teacher, and I was warned about quoting too much. It took effort, but I forced myself to summarize or paraphrase. Believe it or not, I ended up saying more in fewer words, writing more suitably for my own research paper. By getting away from those quotation note cards, I later found the first draft of my paper much easier to write." Since no more than 20% of a paper should be quoted, taking summary, outline, or paraphrase notes saves time later. And who has time to waste?

CHECKLIST FOR NOTES

You should be able to answer "yes" to each of these questions.

1. Have I used a separate note card for each idea?
2. Have I written on only one side of the card?

3. Have I written in ink?
4. Have I used only abbreviations that will make sense to me later?
5. Does every note card include a number, circled, to indicate its source?
6. Does every note card include a page or paragraph reference?
7. Does every note card include a slug?
8. Have I avoided excessive quotations, using them for less than 20% of my notes?
9. Have I used quotation marks every time I used an author's exact words?
10. Have I punctuated quotations and partial quotations correctly, using brackets, ellipses, and other punctuation marks accurately?
11. When summarizing, have I included only main ideas?
12. When paraphrasing, have I been careful to avoid plagiarism?
13. Have I avoided taking too many notes from only one or two sources?
14. Have I used relevant, timely sources suitable for my topic?
15. Have I taken notes that correspond to my working outline or to my revised working outline?
16. Have I revised my working outline as my reading and note taking suggest?

EXERCISES

Exercise A: *Writing a Quotation Note*

Directions: Molly is writing her paper about the prehistoric Indians' use of earthen mounds. She has found the passage below and wants to glean quotation notes from it. Write two quotation notes that would be appropriate for her paper. Be prepared to defend your choices for quotations.

Passage
Indians have roamed the nation's midsection for over 10,000 years, and archaeologists have divided the span into four so-called "traditions": Paleo-Indian, Archaic, Woodland, and Mississippian. Little is known about the Paleo-Indians except that they lived during the last years of the Pleistocene Ice Age and presumably hunted some of the now-extinct animals of the period. The Archaic tradition, from about 8000 B.C. until about 1000 B.C., was characterized by change in both the environment and the people's behavior. Archaic Indians hunted and gathered, which in

later years enabled them to move their camps only seasonally instead of constantly. The Woodland tradition dated from roughly 1000 B.C. to A.D. 900. Pottery appeared. Some crop cultivation appeared. Specialized rituals, including elaborate burial rituals and burial mounds, appeared. The Mississippian tradition, from A.D. 900 to A.D. 1600, was characterized by permanent communities, cultivation of crops, and a dependable and storable food source—notably maize, beans, and squash. Another part of the Mississippian tradition was flat-surfaced mounds, not for burial as in the Woodland tradition, but for the construction and, therefore, conspicuous location of important political, social, and religious buildings.

Exercise B: Writing a Partial Quotation Note

Directions: Carlton is writing a paper about the culture of the Woodland Indians and wants to use the passage in Exercise A to write a partial quotation note. Write a partial quotation note appropriate for his paper. Be sure to use correct punctuation, including any necessary ellipses or brackets. Be prepared to explain why you used the quoted material you chose and why a partial quotation is better in this case than a full quotation or précis.

Exercise C: Writing a Précis

Directions: Use the passage in Exercise A to write a précis. Remember that your précis should be about one-third the length of the original passage, which is roughly 180 words.

Exercise D: Writing an Outline Note

Directions: Jaylynn is writing a paper about an archaeological excavation near her home and wants her introduction to give a quick historical survey of the four prehistoric traditions described in the passage in Exercise A. Write an outline note appropriate for her use. It should fit in a single 3″ × 5″ note card.

Exercise E: Writing a Paraphrase Note

Directions: Lao is comparing the Mississippian Indian tradition to the Woodland tradition. Although he has other material about the Woodland Indians, he needs the information in the passage in Exercise A about the Mississippians. Using only the final part of the passage about the

Mississippian tradition, write a paraphrase suitable for his paper. Be careful to avoid plagiarism.

Exercise F: *Writing a Combination Note*

Directions: Alex is writing about how the geography of his home state of Illinois had attracted prehistoric Indians. Use the passage in Exercise A to write a combination note. You may combine any two techniques you think most suitable for this passage and Alex's purpose. Be prepared to defend your choice of techniques.

8

Studying a
Model Excerpt

*The Importance of
Good Note Taking*

Now that you understand the note-taking process, you are ready to see how the notes become the paper. Such a study will help you more fully appreciate the importance of the note-taking task. Remember that while your working outline guides your note taking, your notes will be the skeleton for your actual paper. In other words, the support for your ideas must come from your resources, either primary or secondary. Thus, before you begin taking notes, study the following excerpt from one of the complete model research papers in Chapter 14. The excerpt illustrates how notes become text and provides a clear picture of the purpose your notes serve.

The following excerpt shows Sarah's note cards on the left-hand page and the resulting text on the right. Pointers regarding Sarah's notes and resulting text appear alongside.

20 14

Wildlife

Public pays attention to endangered species like pandas and grizzlies, but the germline ——"the general genetic heritage, especially of lesser organisms that form the majority — ought to concern us more."

(germline most likely in swamps)

Water table

14 n.p.

Wetlands = hydrologic modifiers
Calls wetlands storage places for water
"They temporarily stockpile water and then release it slowly into streams, thereby keeping floods and droughts from being so exaggerated."

Water table value

14 n.p.

$1.78 trillion — what wetlands are worth in terms of flooding or drought.

EXCERPT FROM

Wetlands: Of What Value?

. . . .

In terms of wildlife in general, Gregg Easterbrook points out that while the public pays attention to endangered species like pandas and grizzlies, they ignore the "germline," a word he coined to refer to "the general genetic heritage especially of lesser organisms that form the majority" (41) of other organisms. The germline, most likely found in swamps, should concern Earth citizens even more than the individual endangered species, for whatever happens to animals soon happens to humankind.

Wetlands, however, do more than protect living plants and animals. They also store water and then release it slowly, reducing the impact of floods and droughts, a function some authorities claim is worth $1.78 trillion to Earth's citizens ("How Much"). Because giant parking lots, acres of buildings, masses of concrete, and many square miles of pavement literally waterproof the land, rainwater cannot soak in, so it is concentrated in large runoffs.

Quotation comes directly from note card; last part paraphrased in separate sentence for emphasis

Quotation from note card paraphrased in Sarah's text

Two note cards incorporated into one sentence

Idea on note card expanded slightly in text

Water table   (26) 4

We've covered the land with buildings, roads, and parking lots. Rain can't soak in, so it runs off, concentrating "large volumes of precipitation."

Water table (26) 7

(discussing a 1-acre swamp)
"If flooded to a depth of one foot, it would hold 330,000 gallons of water. Thus, whenever a swamp is filled or drained, another large quantity of water is lost from the underground water supply and made to run off more quickly to aggravate flooding problems downstream."

Water table

Poole
(interview)

All feel results of wetlands destruction, especially from droughts and floods.

"We _all_ live downstream."

Water filter, value (14) n.p.

Wetlands= filtering system
(like human's kidney function)

Value: $1.70 trillion

Floods result. On the other hand, a one-acre swamp with only a foot of water will retain 330,000 gallons. Thus, every time a wetland is destroyed, the environment is dealt a double blow. First, the area's underground water supply diminishes; second, area runoff increases, thereby escalating downstream flooding (Goodwin and Niering 7). As wetlands biologist Keith Poole explained in a personal interview, "We all live downstream."

The loss of wetlands also results in the loss of nature's filtering systems. Wetlands can remove sediments and pollutants like giant kidneys, a natural service some scientists value at upward of $1.70 trillion ("How Much"). They sponge up the pollutants such as the heavy metals and agricultural runoff, consequently preventing these toxic materials from flowing into fragile estuaries and bays. In fact,

> Quotation carries no special force, so it is paraphrased

> Rewording of sentence adds emphasis by distinguishing two-part results

> Four-word quotation from interview carries impact as concluding sentence

> Examples in text clarify "heavy metals" and "agricultural runoff"

Water filter ⑨ 1

As filters, wetlands can absorb heavy metals and agriculture runoff.

① of ②   ⑨   1

Water filter

4 parts: ① settling pond, ② marsh, ③ pond, ④ meadow

① solid waste broken down
② supplies "natural filter of cattails and bulrushes, where microbes feed off nitrogen and phosphorous, breaking them down to substances readily absorbed by plants" MORE

---

② of ②

Water filter

⑨   1-2

③ Algae feed on "any remaining nutrients as the clean water flows through a filter of grasses"
④ stream water — clean enough to include healthy fish, plants, birds

---

Water filter

㉛   n.p.

"Artificial wetlands now take the place of sewage treatment facilities in almost 150 communities across the U.S."

Also 50 - 90% cheaper

wetlands can even filter sewage. The natural vegetation of a marsh, like cattails and bulrushes, creates a natural filter. Then algae feed on whatever particles are left while grasses function as a filter for the clean water (Lorion 1). In reality, wetlands are so effective at cleaning water that nearly 150 communities, including San Diego and Disney World, use artificial wetlands instead of traditional sewage treatment plants. In so doing, they reap a 50% to 90% savings while creating wildlife refuges at the same time. The stream waters flowing out of such wetlands are cleaner than most municipally treated water and teem with fish, plants,

Text summarizes detailed note cards to explain how swamps filter sewage

Some facts taken from two other sources on sewage treatment

Water filter ③ n.p.

As filter, wetlands remove pollutants, sediments. Plants like water hyacinths efficient at cleaning sewage. Used in San Diego and Disney World.

Water filter   Poole
(interview)

Wetlands are great purifiers so "if you drink water, you suffer."

That's all of us!

and birds ("Wetlands Clean"). To destroy wetlands, then, is to

remove nature's kidneys. As Poole explained, "If you drink water,

you suffer" when wetlands are lost.

Quotation from a primary source for emphasis

As you can see, a paper almost writes itself if you have taken good notes and have taken them according to your working outline. Sarah's notes illustrate some important lessons:

- Students tend to take down too many quotations, which they later must paraphrase or condense. No paper should include strings of quotations.
- You may not use everything on every note card, but it is much more comfortable to have too much information than too little.
- Ideas and information on note cards can be expanded for greater emphasis and support of your thesis.
- Likewise, ideas and information on note cards can be condensed for less emphasis.
- Whatever appears on your note cards will make up the meat of your paper; the support for your body paragraphs comes from your notes.
- Sentences that do not come directly or indirectly from note cards are structural: transitional words, phrases, and sentences, or topic sentences and concluding sentences. Occasionally even concluding sentences can come from carefully selected notes.

Writing the Final Outline

9

Your working outline guided your note taking. No doubt you have made many changes in the outline since you wrote those first lists in Chapter 2. You have probably added numerous subheadings, taken out some others, and may have rearranged a few. Now you are ready to create a final outline, the outline that will guide you in creating your first draft. Remember, however, that even though we are calling this the "final" outline, it still may go through changes during the actual writing process. If it does, simply come back to this chapter to be sure your changes are logical and structurally sound.

Some students cringe at the thought of creating a formal outline with its peculiar combination of Roman and Arabic numerals, uppercase and lowercase letters, formal indentations, and periods. Others see nothing strange at all about the outline format, but they write the paper first and then try to generate an outline from it. Somewhere, somehow these poor souls have been misled about outlines. An outline is nothing more than a plan for your paper. It maps out for you (and sometimes for your reader) what will happen and in what order it will happen. It is a guide to get from here—with this pile of note cards in front of you—to there, the completed paper.

CHOOSING THE FORM

Research papers generally call for topic outlines, and that is what this chapter addresses. Occasionally, however, sentence outlines are required. Quite simply, a sentence outline follows the same logic and the same configuration as a topic outline except that each heading and subheading must be a complete sentence. To be accurate, the sentences must also maintain parallelism; that is, all the sentences in a particular section should have the same grammatical structure. Because of the tedium in creating such grammatically precise outlines, most writers prefer—and most educators accept—the simpler topic outline form.

WRITING THE THESIS STATEMENT

Outlines, either sentence or topic, begin with a thesis statement. Your first step in creating your final outline, then, is to generate your thesis statement.

When you first selected your topic as part of Chapter 1, you phrased your narrowed topic as a question. Your research question helped you create your working outline, directed your research, and determined your note taking. As a result, by now you should have an answer to that research question, and the one-sentence answer is your thesis statement. Compare these research questions with their respective thesis statements:

Question: What are the effects on the environment when wetlands are destroyed?

THESIS: When wetlands are destroyed, for whatever reason, the reduction of the water table affects life of all kinds, even that of the average city dweller.

Question: How did Steinbeck's depiction of the Great Depression in *The Grapes of Wrath* compare with historical and personal experiences?

THESIS: While Steinbeck's depiction of the Great Depression in *The Grapes of Wrath* bears historical accuracy, at least one family showed little similarity between its life and that of the Joads.

Question: What is being done to solve the problem of homelessness?

THESIS: Government, private organizations, and individuals are all working to solve what seems to be the insurmountable problem of homelessness.

Question: What therapeutic effects can come from subliminal perceptions?

THESIS: Subliminal perceptions can aid in the reduction of stress-related problems as simple as weight loss or as complicated as surgery.

Question: How are robotics affecting national industries?

THESIS: Robotics of low, medium, and high technology have revolutionized industry by making it less dependent on but also safer for humans.

Your thesis statement is a kind of summary or description of what your paper is about. Note the following characteristics of these thesis statements.

- Each is a single declarative sentence, not a question.
- Each states the writer's position or findings on the topic.
- Each states the specific focus the paper will have.
- Each suggests what the conclusion will say.
- Each presumably reflects what the writer's notes provide.
- None begins with "The purpose of this paper is . . ." nor states the purpose in any other way. (Compare with "Stating the Purpose" in Chapter 2.)
- Each has only a single main clause.
- None is a statement of the topic.

You may need to rewrite your thesis statement several times before it expresses precisely what your paper will discuss.

SORTING NOTES

You have a stack of note cards. Each has a slug from the working outline. Work through your materials this way:

Step 1: *Sort the note cards according to their slugs.* When Sarah sorted her note cards, she had stacks labeled "Definition," "Loss," "Causes of Destruction," "Fish," "Fowl," "Water Storage," "Water Filter," "Value," etc. The slugs—or labels—came from her working outline.

TECH TIP

If you saved your notes in files titled by slugs, print out a hard copy of each file. Your notes will be automatically sorted!

Step 2: *Check your note cards for slugs not on your outline.* If you have a stack of note cards labeled with a slug that isn't on your outline, you may need to add a heading or subheading. On the other hand, you may simply have some irrelevant information.

CRITICAL THINKING HINT

Analyze how—or if—these additional notes will support your thesis. Are they main ideas? Are they supporting details, statistics, examples, or anecdotes that will explain main ideas? Are they irrelevant?

Avoid the following two temptations:

1. It's tempting to include note cards simply because you have them. Don't!
2. It's tempting to add illogical headings or subheadings to the outline in order to use otherwise irrelevant note cards. Don't!

An illogical addition can destroy your paper's unity or organization. Think before you act.

Step 3: Check outline topics for which you have no note cards. If you have headings or subheadings in your outline for which you have no note cards, you need either to change your outline or return to the library for additional information.

CRITICAL THINKING HINT

Be cautious about eliminating a heading or subheading from your working outline simply because you have no note cards for it. Will removing it leave a hole in your paper? Do you really need to address this issue in order to support your thesis or your main ideas? Before you make changes in your outline, analyze their effects on your final paper.

CHECKING CONTENT

Your outline must reveal a logical organizational pattern and reflect what the thesis statement summarizes. The sum of the parts must equal the whole. Let's see what all this means in terms of a specific example.

Ardys backpacked across Isle Royale, an island national park in Lake Superior where near-arctic winters leave the wilderness deserted. In spite of its inhospitable climate, however, she learned that for many decades people have tried to survive there, and she wondered how—and why. The topic is stated in Ardys's research question: Historically, what means of livelihood attracted people to Isle Royale? The thesis statement, which also answers her research question, summarizes the contents of her paper and sets the tone: words like *battle, isolation,* and *frigid climate* suggest her attitude.

Thesis statement: Only three natural resources have merited people's battle with Isle Royale's isolation and frigid climate.

I. Timber
    A. Destroyed by flood
    B. Devastated by fire

II. Fish
    A. Commercial catches
    B. Individual catches
        1. Decline by unknown causes
        2. Decline by human-made causes

III. Copper
    A. Indian miners
        1. Seasonal activity
        2. Prized results
    B. European settlers
        1. Permanent settlement
        2. Business disaster

Reflecting the Thesis

In Ardys's outline, the three main headings—timber, fish, and copper—when added together equal the thesis statement. They name the "three natural resources." Under "Timber," the two subheadings, "Destroyed by flood" and "Devastated by fire," represent the two kinds of battles waged to gain wealth from the lumber. Likewise, items 1 and 2, "Decline by unknown causes" and "Decline by human-made causes," represent the relatively equal subheadings about individual fishing that declined as a result of these two causes. Note how, in each category, the subheadings, taken together, equal their main headings. The outline moves from the general to the specific.

CRITICAL THINKING HINT

The relationship between an outline and a paper can be represented by the following mathematical equations:

1. All main headings together are the equivalent of the thesis: I + II + III + IV = Thesis
2. A heading with its subheadings is the equivalent of a paragraph with its supporting details: I = A + B or A = 1 + 2

Revealing an Organizational Pattern

The order in which headings and subheadings are listed is not a matter of coincidence. You must have a reason for choosing the order, and that reason is guided by your purpose. Consider these examples:

Kurt's paper will discuss the potential applications of voice synthesizers and voice recognition by computers, so he will organize his paper from the most realistic applications to the most hypothetical, hoping to stimulate his reader's imagination.

Cassandra's paper is a cause-effect topic analyzing the use and dangers of nitrates in food, so she will first use chronological order (nitrates must be added to food before they can pose a threat) to give background. That will be followed by a discussion of the dangerous effects of nitrates arranged by order of importance from least to most dangerous.

Julio's paper will examine the water crisis in the Southwest by tracing the causes leading to the present situation, so he will organize his paper chronologically.

Juan's paper will summarize the most tantalizing discoveries of *Voyager II*, so he will use a spatial order, moving across the solar system with *Voyager*.

Each student chose a pattern of organization that will best support his or her purpose and topic. The most common organizational patterns include

- chronological order
- spatial order
- order of importance

The order of importance incorporates three alternatives:

- from most important to least important (best for newspaper articles that the reader may not finish)
- from second most important to least important to most important (best for persuasive papers assuming an antagonistic reader)

- from least important to most important (commonly used for general work, including research papers)

(Note that this list is organized from least to most important for research writers.)

In Ardys's outline on page 162, she uses the order of importance from least to most important. Her research showed that timber was the least profitable natural resource and had the least impact on settlement of the island; copper, even though it was also a business disaster, was the most profitable and had the greatest impact. Within the divisions, however, she varies the organization. She arranges the subheadings for all three categories chronologically. In other words, the earliest lumber business was destroyed by floods, but later business was wiped out after forest fires destroyed the timber.

In summary, revise your own outline as necessary to include these two logical characteristics:

1. Your outline must reflect the thesis; a summary of its parts must equal the thesis statement.
2. Your outline must reveal a logical organizational pattern.

CHECKING STRUCTURE

Look again at Ardys's outline. Note the following characteristics:

1 *The outline follows the standard format.* The outline correctly follows the standard number-letter format with appropriate capitalization and punctuation. Outlines alternate numbers and letters in the following order:

> Roman numerals: I, II, III, IV, V, etc.
> Uppercase letters: A, B, C, D, E, etc.
> Arabic numerals: 1, 2, 3, 4, 5, etc.
> Lowercase letters: a, b, c, d, e, etc.
> Arabic numerals with parentheses: (1), (2), (3), etc.
> Lowercase letters with parentheses: (a), (b), etc.

Remember, however, that an outline that goes into fifth or sixth levels probably has one of two problems: it is too detailed, or its main categories are too broad. Even fourth-level subheadings represent an idea that will be developed with specific details, examples, or illustrations. A subheading must never represent only a single sentence in a paragraph.

The outline also uses proper capitalization and punctuation. Note the following:

- Only the first word in a heading or subheading of a topic outline is capitalized, except, of course, proper nouns or adjectives, which are always capitalized.
- A period follows each letter or number in the outline configuration except in the fifth and sixth levels where parentheses are used.
- No period follows headings or subheadings in a topic outline.
- The ragged left margin permits the vertical alignment of the periods following the Roman numerals.
- The pattern of indentation properly spaces letters and numbers.

2 *The number of subheadings is about equal.* The fact that Ardys has used a nearly equal number of subheadings in each section shows careful division. For instance, part III is divided into A, with two subheadings, and B, also with two subheadings. To have, for example, six subheadings under A and none under B or eight subheadings under II and two under III would probably suggest an illogical division.

CRITICAL THINKING HINT

Logically, no part of an outline can have fewer than two subheadings. After all, how can anything be divided into fewer than two? Thus, no outline can have an A without a B or a 1 without a 2. For example, in the sample outline on page 162, if the timber industry were never affected by flood but only destroyed by fire, the subheadings A and B would be eliminated entirely. The writer would address the fire destruction of the timber industry as a single point, outlined as Roman numeral I. The wording of Roman numeral I would, of course, have to remain parallel with other like divisions of the outline.

WRONG: I. Timber
               A. Destroyed by fire
      II. Fish
               A. Commercial catches
               B. Individual catches

RIGHT (Okay):   I. Timber
                II. Fish
                     A. Commercial catches
                     B. Individual catches

RIGHT (Better):   I. Timber destroyed by fire
                II. Fish destroyed by overharvests
                     A. Commercial catches
                     B. Individual catches

3 *The headings are mutually exclusive.* "Mutually exclusive" means that subheadings do not overlap one another or merely rename the preceding heading. The following excerpts illustrate:

ILLOGICAL   I. College students
                    A. Male
                    B. Female
                    C. Older

This outline segment suggests that older students are neither male nor female, but some other gender.

LOGICAL   I. College students
                    A. Traditional
                       1. Male
                       2. Female
                    B. Nontraditional
                       1. Male
                       2. Female

4 *The means of division are logical.* An example best illustrates logical and illogical divisions. If pies are divided into the following categories, the divisions are illogical:

- homemade
- best restaurant
- fruit
- recipes

Instead, divide by a single criterion:

- by where they are made: homemade, restaurant purchased, or bakery purchased
- by their contents: fruit, custard, meat
- by their quality in restaurants: poor, good, better, best
- by their preparation: whole baked, cooked filling, nonbaked

5 *The topics within a division are parallel.* Parallelism refers to the use of like grammatical structures. Notice the following examples of parallel structures in Ardys's outline on page 162:

- Single-word nouns make up the three parallel main headings.
- Past participles with prepositional phrases make up the parallel sub-headings A and B in part I.
- Adjectives with nouns form parallel subheadings A and B in part II.
- Nouns with prepositional phrases form parallel subheadings 1 and 2 under part II B.

All topics within a level must be parallel to each other. Thus, in Ardys's outline, A and B in part I are parallel to each other, but they are not parallel to A and B in part III. However, A and B in part III must be—and are—parallel to each other.

6 *The outline maps out the body of the paper.* Formal outlines for research papers omit the headings "Introduction" and "Conclusion." Of course, those components are part of the paper, but they do not appear on the outline. Only the body paragraphs are represented by the outline.

Although we do not have Ardys's complete paper, we can guess from her outline how her paper will be written. In general, paragraphs are represented in the outline by uppercase letters. Supporting details for those paragraphs are represented by the subheadings. Thus, her paper will probably have six body paragraphs, corresponding to the six uppercase letters in her outline. Sometimes, in a longer paper, subheadings themselves represent full paragraphs.

TIME MANAGEMENT GUIDELINES

Since writing the final outline should be nothing more than revising and polishing, spend no more than a single day on the effort, no matter how much time you have for the completion of the final paper.

TWO STUDENTS' PROGRESS

Both Sarah and Terry found writing the final outline a comparatively easy process:

Sarah

My final outline looked really different from that sketchy thing I wrote as a first working outline (page 32) or even the revised outline that evolved as I took notes (pages 143–144). I had some rearranging to do to show logical order in the way I listed the effects, and that turned out to be my biggest headache. There didn't seem to be much reason for listing one effect before or after another, so I arranged them from the most obvious to the least. I decided that in this case I needed to start with the familiar and move to the less familiar in order to help my reader follow more easily.

I guess parallelism was the only other problem I faced. Some of the headings just didn't seem to want to conform! But it all worked out. Mostly it was a matter of coming up with the right words, and the thesaurus helped. So did the thesaurus on my computer! The truth of it, though, is that when several of us in class sat down together to work on our outlines, my classmates made suggestions that really helped me get the whole thing parallel. Someone else will see your problem differently, and I'm convinced that's the trick to solving really sticky parallelism problems!

So here's my final outline, beginning with my thesis statement:

Thesis Statement: When the earth's citizens recognize wetlands' values, perhaps they will be more concerned about the protection of those vanishing areas.

I. Definitions of wetlands
   A. Definition by category
   B. Definition by characteristics
   C. Definition by law

II. Destruction of wetlands
   A. Losses
      1. Past
      2. Continuing
   B. Causes

III. Effects of destruction
   A. On plant life
   B. On animal life
      1. Marine creatures
      2. Waterfowl
      3. Other wildlife

   C. On water
      1. Storage area
      2. Filtering system

    D. On biosphere
IV. Value to humans
    A. Economic impact
    B. Economic controversy
    C. Resulting efforts

Terry

My working outline was the pits! By the time I did the interview and all my reading, however, the outline was taking on good form. Even though my final outline was really short, it was adequate for my 900-word paper.

Thesis Statement: In spite of the two families' similar circumstances, the Gishes felt less than a tremor of the economic quake that shook the fictional lives of the Joads.

  I. Religious faith
    A. Strong beliefs
    B. Difficult circumstances
 II. Family unity
    A. Gish family
    B. Joad family
III. Racial background
    A. White Joads
    B. Biracial Gishes

TIPS AND TRAPS

Most student errors in outlining come from muddy thinking. When you finish your outline, try Sarah's little trick for checking your logic: "Start at the bottom of your outline. Look at the items in the last division and decide if they add up to their main heading. Then look at the items in the next division and make the same check. If 1 + 2 + 3 doesn't equal C—or whatever—then something is wrong. That's how we checked each other's outlines in my class, and I was surprised at how well that little trick worked!" And remember that another person's objective check of your work will often turn up something you have not thought about yourself. That person's distance from your topic makes him or her more objective than you can be.

Of course, mechanical details—periods, spacing, capital letters, and so forth—are also important, so double-check them as well.

CHECKLIST FOR THE FINAL OUTLINE

As you evaluate your own outline, you should be able to answer "yes" to each of these questions.

1. Does my outline reflect my thesis, i.e., does the sum of the parts equal the thesis statement?
2. Did I choose an organizational pattern that will best reflect my purpose and my topic?
3. Does my outline reveal the logical organizational pattern for my paper?
4. Have I divided the topics into relatively equal parts?
5. Have I avoided the illogical use of a subheading designated A without one designated B or a 1 without a 2?
6. Have I used headings and subheadings that are mutually exclusive?
7. Have I used logical divisions?
8. Have I avoided fifth- and sixth-level divisions for which I have nothing more than a sentence to write?
9. Does my outline maintain parallel structure?
10. Does my outline follow the conventions for punctuation, indentation, and capitalization as follows:
    a. Are Roman numerals arranged so the periods align?
    b. Is each letter in second-level divisions capitalized and followed by a period?
    c. Are Arabic numbers in third-level divisions followed by periods?
    d. Does each heading and subheading begin with an uppercase letter, and the other words (except proper nouns and adjectives) begin with lowercase letters?
    e. Have I omitted periods after headings and subheadings?

EXERCISES

Exercise A: *Choosing a Logical Order*

Directions: Arrange the four or five items in these groups in some logical order. Name the basis of the arrangement and be prepared to explain why you would use that arrangement. (You may choose variations of the organizational patterns listed in this chapter.)

1. hall runner, doormat, area rug, wall-to-wall carpet
2. suit and tie, shorts and tank top, slacks and sport shirt, jeans and T-shirt

3. plums, oranges, bananas, apples, grapes
4. St. Louis, New York, Chicago, Miami, Los Angeles
5. Nile, Mississippi, Amazon, Ohio, Danube
6. football, golf, baseball, basketball, soccer
7. radio, television, newspapers, magazines
8. denim, oxford cloth, corduroy, chambray
9. Neil Simon, William Shakespeare, Tennessee Williams, Arthur Miller
10. Pluto, Jupiter, Neptune, Mercury, Earth
11. Norway, Peru, Israel, Egypt, Bangladesh
12. bicycle, airplane, train, automobile, ship

Exercise B: Creating an Outline

Directions: Use the following headings and subheadings to generate an accurate topic outline. If arranged correctly, the topics will be parallel. Be sure to insert necessary punctuation, capitalization, indentation, and other configurations appropriate to a topic outline. (Note: You may find more than one order suitable for this outline. Be able to defend your logical choice.)

employer action
at the workplace
improved ventilation
effects of secondhand smoke
on mates
individual action
enticing incentives
class-action suits
on children
governmental legislation
legal action
at home
solutions to secondhand smoke
separate facilities

Exercise C: Analyzing an Outline

Directions: The following topic outline includes a number of problems. Write a list identifying both logical and structural errors.

Thesis Statement: The purpose of this paper is to show how lasers have affected modern life.

  I. Medical
     A. Surgery dangers
        1. Damage
     B. Surgery recovery
        1. at the hospital
        2. at home
     C. Stay

 II. Military
     A. Detection
        1. Peacetime
        2. Launch
     B. Tracking
     C. Identification
     D. Firing
        1. Destroy
           a. Directed-energy weapons
           b. Kinetic-energy weapons

10

Writing the Draft

So here you sit, blank page (or blank screen) in front of you. You have read, taken notes, stacked your note cards by topic, written and rewritten outlines. Now it is time to write The Paper. And maybe you feel a wave of panic, cold sweat, or just a knot in your stomach.

No need for any of that. Remember that your notes contain all the information you need and your outline lays out the organization. All you have to do is write, and the more quickly you get the first draft on paper, the better. In fact, it is best to set aside a single block of time and complete the draft in one sitting (or, if your paper is long, at least complete an entire section in one sitting). As you write, write fast, not worrying about spelling, mechanics, or usage problems. Think only about ideas. Get them down as quickly as possible. You will revise and proofread later.

GENERAL SUGGESTIONS

Although every writer works differently, the following general suggestions may prove helpful.

1   *Use ink.* Even though you will make changes as you write your first draft, you can do that with cross-outs, arrows, or insertions. Erasing pencil will leave smears, even holes; and if you use pencil, the draft will eventually smear, perhaps obliterating your work.

2 *Write on one side of the paper on every other line.* Later, if you need to cut and paste to reorganize, you can easily do so. If you write only on every other line, the extra space allows you to make more legible additions, changes, or deletions.

TECH TIP

If you are accustomed to writing at the keyboard and can type faster than you can write by hand, try doing your first draft on the computer. Be sure, however, to set the page format for double-spaced lines. Since you will no doubt revise both on screen and on copy, double-spacing will ease the task.

3 *Throw away nothing.* To pitch a note card is to guarantee you will need it later. To throw away all or part of an early draft is to make certain something on it will later prove essential. Instead, use a large envelope for what at the moment seems like trash. You will have the "trash" out of your way but not gone forever.

4 *Stay on track and follow your outline.* Some beginning writers seem to forget why they created the outline and wander off on some tangent. Follow its organizational pattern. You'll know if it needs to be changed when you read your draft.

The following sections discuss the three basic parts of the paper: the introduction, body, and conclusion. We will look at ways to work most successfully through the first draft of these parts.

INTRODUCTION

We have already acknowledged that every writer works differently, so you will not be surprised to learn that some writers write the introduction last. It may, indeed, be easier to dive right in with the first point on your outline. If that is your preference, come back to this section when you are ready to write your introduction.

The introduction must set the stage for your paper. "Setting the stage" means that, first, the introduction should prepare readers for what they are about to read. Use your own words, for rarely will anyone else's words address your specific focus. Second, the introduction should set the tone for the topic, your purpose, and your thesis. If the introduction is humorous, your reader expects a humorous paper. Third, for some topics the introduction may also include background information and definitions of technical or abstract terms. Avoid, however, insulting your reader with simple definitions like "Webster's defines democracy as . . ." Fourth, the introduction usually concludes with your thesis statement, either stated or implied. In the case of a persuasive paper likely to be read by an antagonistic audience, however, the thesis statement may be postponed until the conclusion.

CRITICAL THINKING HINT

In order to write the most effective introduction, think about your topic and your purpose. Your introduction should reflect both. The introduction sets the tone—informative, persuasive, whatever. Thus, you cannot consider the suggestions here as a "formula" for an introduction with so many sentences that introduce and a final sentence that states the thesis. Use the most effective means available to prepare your audience to read and understand your paper. To do that, put yourself in your readers' shoes. Analyze their needs in terms of your message.

The research paper, in spite of its rather formidable reputation, profits from a creative introduction, especially one that draws in readers and somehow personally involves them in your subject. Perhaps one of the following common kinds of introductions will work for your paper:

1 *Startle the reader with facts or statistics.* Carmen is writing a paper about how the U.S. national debt will affect her generation, so she wants her readers to understand how much a trillion dollars is. Her introduction begins this way: "If a person could count twenty-four hours a day, it would take 31,688 years to count to a trillion." Jason is writing a paper that will explain some of the theories of plate tectonics. His introduction begins with this surprising fact: "The highest mountain in the world is not, in fact, Mount Everest. Another mountain, over 4,000 feet higher but partly submerged in the vast depths of the Pacific Ocean, claims that record. The title rightfully belongs to Mauna Kea on the island of Hawaii, part of the largest mountain range in the world." Both writers startle their readers and, simultaneously, pique their interest.

2 *Describe a compelling condition or situation.* Sarah describes a compelling situation in her paper on wetlands. She begins this way: "Quaking bogs and snake-infested, mosquito-ridden swamps make up the stuff of chiller movies where the gooey slime hides both crime and criminal and the gloom is home to creepy crawly things." She knows readers can identify with this typical reaction to wetlands.

3 *Use a story or conversation to introduce an event.* Dantiele is writing a paper about Russian economic problems in the past and wants his readers to understand the unavailability of goods at that time. He introduces his paper with a story about Yvette: "At the bakery, Yvette stood in line for two hours this morning. She wanted a loaf of bread for her three children, her husband, and herself. Just one loaf. When she finally reached the head of the line, a weary clerk told her, 'No more bread. Try tomorrow.'" Dantiele has let his readers identify with ordinary Russian citizens.

4 *Explain a conflict or inconsistency.* Lana is writing a paper about energy conservation. To involve her readers personally, she begins with this seeming inconsistency: "Perhaps it sounds like a Ripley's believe-it-or-not fact, but shaving with a hand razor uses more electricity than does shaving with an electric razor." Surprised by this apparent inconsistency, readers want to know how this is possible. When they finish, they learn that pumps that keep the water flowing use more electricity than does a small razor.

5 *Ask a question.* Glenna is writing about the influence of Socrates on question-answer strategies in teaching and has chosen a thought-provoking question to engage her readers: "How can it be that the great teacher Socrates never wrote a word, that all we know of his teachings is from his student Plato?" Readers assume she will answer that question in the course of her paper.

6 *Use a quotation, adage, or proverb.* Jeff is writing a literary paper analyzing Ezra Pound's early poetry. His introduction begins with a quotation: " 'Great literature is simply language charged with meaning to the utmost possible degree.' So said Ezra Pound." The quotation attracts reader interest, and Jeff will use the idea of "charged with meaning to the utmost" as the basis for the poetic analysis.

Other methods may work just as well to introduce your paper, but these six suggestions should at least spark an idea.

TEMPORARY DOCUMENTATION

As you write the first draft, you must—absolutely must—keep track of which information comes from which sources. You might remember these two warnings from Chapter 7:

1. Be sure you list the source and page number for all information.
2. Be sure to enclose the exact words of a source in quotation marks.

Which information in your paper needs documentation? In short, anything that comes from either a primary or secondary resource:

Document

- quotations or partial quotations
- others' ideas, even if in your words
- others' opinions, even if in your words
- little-known facts, even if easily proven

Do Not Document

- your personal opinions and interpretations
- well-known facts

The difference between well-known facts and little-known facts can be a matter of debate, but consider these examples: Virtually everyone knows that Abraham Lincoln was assassinated while serving as United States President, so that fact or the date and place of the deed need not be documented. On the other hand, not everyone knows that Robert Todd Lincoln, son of Abraham Lincoln, witnessed the assassinations of three presidents—his father's, President Garfield's, and President McKinley's—and, as a result, refused to attend any more state affairs. That curious fact, although rather readily verified, would need documentation.

In short, follow this rule: If in doubt, document. Better safe than sorry.

Now that you are transferring information from your note cards to your first draft, you must take pains not to lose track of this documentation. Here are the quickest, simplest ways to stay out of trouble:

1 *From each note card, list the source and page numbers in parentheses.* For example, Sarah wrote the following in her first draft:

Wetlands can remove sediments and pollutants like giant

kidneys. (10:2)

The parenthetical numbers came from her note card and represent the source (the bibliography card she has numbered 10) and the page (2) in that source. The source number is followed by a colon, and additional page numbers are separated with hyphens (for consecutive pages) or commas (for nonconsecutive pages):

> 10:2–5 (source 10, pages 2 through 5)
> 10:2, 5 (source 10, pages 2 and 5)

2 *Before you finish with a note card, check for quotation marks.* If the note card is a quotation or partial quotation, be absolutely certain that you include the quotation marks in your draft. To forget or carelessly omit quotation marks around the exact words from a source is to plagiarize. Remember the serious penalties for literary theft and BE CAREFUL.

BODY PARAGRAPHS

You know how to develop a paragraph; you have been writing paragraphs for years. Since the body of a research paper is nothing more than a series of paragraphs, you should have no difficulty writing it. As a reminder, however, review these general guidelines for developing body paragraphs:

1 *Follow your outline.* You have already grouped your note cards according to slugs that correspond to outline headings. Although you can begin with any major outline heading (those marked with Roman numerals) and the corresponding stack of note cards, most writers start with the first. Your outline indicates paragraph divisions. For instance, everything under Roman numeral 1 may be a single paragraph. Terry's paper illustrates such an approach. (See Chapter 14.) Likewise, it is possible—even probable for a longer paper—that the first-level divisions (those designated by uppercase letters) or even second-level divisions (those designated by Arabic numbers) represent single paragraphs. Sarah's paper illustrates this approach. (See Chapter 14.)

Notice how the following segment of Sarah's outline translates into paragraphs:

III. Effects of destruction
    A. On plant life   One paragraph with this topic sentence: Exploring the destruction of that resource leads first to the wide variety of plant life supported by wetlands. . . .

B. On animal life
    1. Marine life

One paragraph with this topic sentence: The other half [of the effect of wetlands destruction] belongs to animal life, beginning with marine creatures.

    2. Waterfowl

One paragraph with this topic sentence: The situation is just as serious for waterfowl.

    3. Other wildlife

One paragraph with this topic sentence: In terms of wildlife in general, Gregg Easterbrook points out that . . .

C. On water
    1. Storage area

One paragraph with this topic sentence: [Wetlands] also store water and then release it slowly. . . .

    2. Filtering system

One paragraph with this topic sentence: The loss of wetlands also results in the loss of nature's filtering system.

D. On biosphere

One paragraph with this topic sentence: Finally, wetlands also help maintain biospheric stability.

Study the complete models in Chapter 14 to see how outline headings and subheadings dictate paragraphs. (See final outlines on pages 168 and 169.)

2 *Use your note cards to develop support for each paragraph.* Whether you state or imply the topic sentence in each paragraph, remember what you already know about good writing: each paragraph develops and carefully supports a single idea. Because a research paper should reflect what you have learned about a topic, good support is essential.

You have already arranged your note cards in stacks according to outline headings; therefore, you simply need to transfer the notes into the first draft at the appropriate places.

3 *Maintain unity.* Your note cards will provide the specific details for each main idea: facts, statistics, illustrations, anecdotes, examples. Be careful, however, that you do not wander off the topic just because you have some extra note cards. Maybe some of the notes do not belong in the paper.

CRITICAL THINKING HINT

You may be startled to discover at this stage of the writing process that notes you once thought were good are now obviously inappropriate or that you have too little information to develop an idea fully. Stay calm. This problem is common, even among the most experienced researchers. Remember that writing is a recursive process: you will not be positively finished with library research, reading, note taking, and writing until the final draft is finished!

As you work, think. Analyze every paragraph. Does everything in this paragraph support the topic sentence? At the same time, have you included adequate information to support the topic sentence fully? Do you need more facts? Statistics? Some examples? An illustration? If your notes lack the necessary supporting details, plan a return trip to the library.

4 *Blend material from your note cards into your own sentences.* As you incorporate the material from your note cards into your paragraphs, use good transitions and clarifying sentences to connect the specific details, statistics, and examples into a smooth piece of writing. (See examples of how Sarah developed note cards into an early draft in Chapter 8.)

CRITICAL THINKING HINT

When actually writing the first draft of a paper, writers sometimes find that the carefully prepared outline simply does not work. If logic tells you that a different arrangement would be better, change your outline. Remember that nothing is final until you hand in your final draft!

How do you know whether the outline does not work or whether there is some other problem? Ask yourself questions like these:

- Is there a cause-effect relationship here I need to acknowledge in my organization?
- Is there a time relationship that I must recognize?
- Is one topic more (or less) important than I originally thought?

- Now that I see the evidence on paper, do my notes support a different conclusion than I first thought?
- Is this going to make sense to my readers?

TECH TIP

If you took notes on the computer, you may be able to save a great deal of keyboarding time now. Consider these two alternatives:

- Having saved your notes in separate files by slug, you can now copy appropriate files into the text of your first draft, rearrange them as necessary, eliminate repetitious or irrelevant notes, add connecting words, phrases, and sentences, and flesh out the paragraph as necessary.
- If you did not save notes in separate files by slug, you can still use copy and paste to move notes into the text of your paper.

Both steps eliminate the need for retyping note card material. Remember to make frequent backup files as you work.

5 *Blend any quoted material into your own sentences.* Many beginning research writers are tempted to produce papers that are nothing more than a string of quotations. Remember that in most cases no more than 20% of your paper should be quoted material. When you do use quotations, use them smoothly. Write the material both before and after a quotation in such a way that your readers neither hear nor feel a bump in the text. Consider these techniques (and study the model papers in Chapter 14 for additional illustrations):

a. Run a quotation into your own sentence.

> Example: Earlier labeled "the Rodney Dangerfield of the environment" (10:2), wetlands are gaining respect as an integral part of life's interdependence.

> Example: The stream waters flowing out of such wetlands are "cleaner than most municipally treated water" (6:72) and teem with fish, plants, and birds.

b. Credit the source within the text.

    Example: According to environmentalist Malcolm F. Baldwin, the wetland remaining is "less than one-half of 215 million acres" (14:17) of original wetlands.

    Example: As wetlands biologist Keith Poole explained in a personal interview, "We all live downstream."

c. Allow the quotation to stand as its own sentence.

    Example: Along the lower Mississippi valley, only 20% of the wetlands once covered with hardwood forest remains, and an additional 100,000 acres disappear every year. "Since 1950 over 4.5 million acres of wetlands have been lost in the Mississippi flyway alone." (13:43)

d. If all other methods seem inappropriate, use a colon to introduce a long quotation.

    Example: A 1983 Environmental Law Institute publication names seven categories of wetlands losses: "drainage (for crop and timber production) . . ."

6 *Tables and figures must stand alone, but blend references to them into your text.* Tables and figures may be taken directly from secondary sources or compiled from surveys, experiments, or other primary research. Tables show the relationships of numbers: dollars spent by year, automobiles produced by manufacturer, average wind velocities by geographic region. Anything else—a diagram, photograph, drawing, map, chart, graph—is called a figure. Both tables and figures, with their accompanying titles, must be self-explanatory. Your text, however, must refer to them, and their contents must give added support to that paragraph's topic sentence. At the same time, however, your text must be clear *without* the tables or figures.

In order to make clear, concise reference to tables and figures in your text, number them consecutively: Table 1, Figure 1, Table 2, and so forth; and then refer to them by number, not by "the following table" or "the figure below."

TRANSITIONAL DEVICES

As you move from idea to idea, from subheading to another main heading, help your readers move with you. The best means for doing that is to use effective transitions or connecting words. Actually, transitions can be words, phrases, complete sentences, or even full paragraphs. Study these examples from Sarah's paper:

Transitional word:	The loss of wetlands <u>also</u> results in the loss of nature's filtering system.
Transitional phrase:	<u>In fact,</u> the most threatened wetlands are not the big or famous . . .
Transitional sentence:	Depending on how one defines wetlands and depending on whose statistics one reads, anywhere from half to two-thirds of the United States' wetlands have been destroyed.
Transitional paragraph: (excerpt) (See page 241 in the model paper for the complete paragraph.)	[Paragraph just completed discusses massive loss of wetlands.] Given these vast losses, the real question for many is why should anyone care, especially when wetlands are "reviled as mosquito havens" (Youth). . . . Consequently, to destroy wetlands is to destroy a resource for plants and animals from the bottom of the food chain all the way up to humans. [Following paragraph describes the loss of habitat for plants at the bottom of the food chain.]

In general, use transitional words and phrases to connect sentences within a paragraph. Use transitional sentences to join paragraphs. Use transitional paragraphs between major headings. For instance, the sample transitional sentence comes at the beginning of a new paragraph that gives statistics about the amount of wetlands destruction. The previous paragraphs described the struggle for defining wetlands. The sample transitional paragraph comes after the paragraph detailing part II B of Sarah's outline and provides a transition into part III.

The following list represents commonly used transitional words and phrases. Use a thesaurus to find additional choices.

To show time relationships after, afterward, at last, at the same time, before, during, earlier, eventually, finally, first, in the meantime, in time, later, meanwhile, next, once, since, soon, subsequently, then, when, whenever

To show comparison again, also, another, as, at the same time, besides, both, each, equally, either . . . or, furthermore, in addition, in like manner, in the same way, like, likewise, moreover, nevertheless, nonetheless, not only . . . but also, similarly, since, still, too, while

To show contrast although, but, despite, even if, even though, however, in contrast, in spite of, nor, on the one hand, on the other hand, on the contrary, otherwise, unless, yet

To show degree above all, additionally, best, better, even more, further, furthermore, greater, greatest, least, less, more, most, over and above, to a lesser extent, to a smaller degree, worse, worst

To show result or purpose as a result, because, consequently, following that, for, in effect, in order that, in the aftermath, next, owing to, since, subsequent to, subsequently, thus, therefore

To show explanation by way of illustration, for example, for instance, in fact, in other words, specifically, that is, thus, to be specific, to illustrate

CONCLUSION

The conclusion of a research paper, like other concluding paragraphs, should leave readers feeling satisfied that you have fully supported your thesis statement. The most satisfying conclusions say something worthwhile and reflect the introduction, giving the reader the sense of having come full circle. (See the model papers in Chapter 14 for illustrations.)

A concluding paragraph usually follows one of these patterns:

1 *Provides a summary* The conclusion summarizes the main ideas of the paper and adds a wrap-up statement that brings the paper to a close. This kind of conclusion, while often the most logical, tends to lack creativity and, if not well written, may leave readers thinking, "So what?"

2 *Reaches a conclusion* Sometimes the concluding paragraph pulls together the key points of the paper and draws from those points some opinion, judgment, result, agreement, decision, resolution, deduction, or inference.

CRITICAL THINKING HINT

If you use this method of concluding your paper, be certain that your result derives logically from the material in your paper. If results are inconclusive, then you must say so. Above all, do not make concluding remarks for which contradictory evidence exists in your paper; rather, acknowledge the contradiction.

3 *Makes an observation* If your paper makes no effort to reach a conclusion or present an argument, your concluding paragraph may simply make a broad observation about your topic. Terry's paper on Steinbeck's *The Grapes of Wrath* illustrates this kind of conclusion. (See Chapter 14.)

4 *Issues a challenge* Based on supporting material in the paper, a concluding paragraph can issue a challenge to readers. The challenge may be to take some action (seek new legislation, buy recycled products, prepare for nuclear disaster) or to change some action (quit smoking, drive more slowly, get more exercise). Sarah's paper on wetlands issues an indirect challenge. (See Chapter 14.)

5 *Refers to the introduction* If the introduction refers to a striking incident, tells a powerful story, or recounts startling statistics, the conclusion can remind readers of those beginning remarks. For instance, Dantiele began his paper on Russian economic problems with a story about Yvette standing in line waiting to buy bread. By bringing Yvette back to the reader's attention in the conclusion, he can involve readers personally in his final statements. He may write something like this: "Yvette still stands in line for hours every day. She hopes to buy bread, or meat, or some small bunch of produce for her family. While the family never complains, her heart aches that she cannot feed them until they feel full. She wonders who will help her put food on the table."

By writing a conclusion that closes the circle, so to speak, you give readers a sense of completion, a sense of satisfaction in a job well done.

Finally, be sure your concluding paragraph introduces no new issues, no unanswered questions, no otherwise unsupported ideas. A conclusion must only conclude. Powerfully, perhaps dramatically, certainly creatively, it should leave readers with a definite attitude about your topic: happy, frustrated, angry, stimulated, curious, annoyed—or whatever feeling you want them to have.

CRITICAL THINKING HINT

Your attitude toward your topic will affect your readers' attitudes. In other words, if you feel boredom with your subject, chances are your readers will feel the same.

Consciously plan to leave readers with a specific attitude. Analyze what you can do in your writing to leave them with that attitude.

TITLE

Frequently a writer pays too little attention to the title of his or her research paper. With little regard to the message, whatever words or phrases pop into mind appear as a title. But titles can bring smiles or yawns, raise eyebrows or interest. They do matter.

The most sound advice about titles is to choose a straightforward one. Avoid a title that is cute for the sake of being cute. For example, no one can guess what a paper titled "Attention! Halt!" will be about. Is it something military? Something environmental? A safety hazard? A health hazard? A literary analysis of *The Winds of War*? Avoid making your reader guess. Your title should accomplish three purposes:

1. suggest your topic
2. represent your message
3. reflect the tone of your paper

It can be factual: "How Hadley Won the Mayoral Election" or "The Results of Car-Wax Tests on Automotive Paint Surfaces." It can be creative: "The Featherweight as Heavyweight: Tough New Canoe Construction." Select the approach best for your topic and purpose.

TIME MANAGEMENT GUIDELINES

At the beginning of this chapter, we suggested that you write the first draft in one sitting, writing as quickly as possible. The ideal is not always possible, however, so you may need to parcel out time. If so, do plan to write in one sitting at least a complete main idea (designated by a Roman numeral in your outline). Total time for the first draft should not exceed these guidelines:

Number of weeks until final paper is due	Number of days available to write first draft
10	9
8	7
6	5
4	3

TWO STUDENTS' PROGRESS

Procrastination causes beginning research writers untold agony. Perhaps they procrastinate because they simply prefer not to work. Maybe it is because they are afraid of the task at hand. For whatever reason, putting off the writing of the first draft can literally destroy the good effort you have made to this point. Listen to Sarah and Terry as they share their experiences.

Sarah

I write regularly at a computer and am reasonably fast at keyboarding. As a result, writing the first draft probably took me less time than it did my classmates who wrote with pen and paper. In spite of that, for me, writing the draft was just plain hard work. Our teacher said we had everything we needed in our note cards and on our outlines, but the writing wasn't all that simple. There's just so *much* to think about—topic sentences, supporting details, transitions.

I didn't start with the introduction. In fact, I wrote my body paragraphs in order, then the introduction, and finally the conclusion. True, my sentences were choppy, and lots of places had no transition, but I dealt with that later. My purpose in my first draft was only to get ideas down in black and white.

Terry

While I have a computer available, I'm not comfortable writing first drafts at the keyboard. So I took the pen-and-paper route. My outline needed no further revision, so the work moved along rather smoothly.

I wrote my introduction first, then I wrote each section at one sitting. I did that at home in the evening when I work best. Then I did the conclusion. Since my paper has five paragraphs, that means I spent five evenings writing. As I wrote, I included the full documentation. My biggest mistake was writing on both sides of my paper. That habit comes from trying to be conservation-minded, not wasting paper. Here, though, I could have benefited by being able to cut the paper apart and paste in new sections. Next time, I'll write only on one side!

TIPS AND TRAPS

While every writer has his or her own working style, most beginning research writers find writing a long paper much different from writing a short one. Shawn offers one suggestion you may find helpful: Start each new main idea on a new sheet of paper. "I was quickly aware of any imbalance in main ideas using this technique," he explained. For instance, if one main idea is detailed in a half page and the next main idea takes four pages, you may have illogical main divisions. More likely, however, you simply lack adequate development for one main idea. Shawn continues illustrating why he likes the new-idea-new-page approach: "Your readers aren't just plowing through a list of ideas; they need to see the relationships among those ideas. So, as our teacher explained, strong transitions have to say to readers, 'You've finished reading about this main idea; I'm moving to the next idea.' The page divisions forced me to see where I needed those strong transitions."

You will need to employ rather strict self-discipline in order to complete the first draft in an appropriate time frame. There are always those students who wait until the eleventh hour, stay up all night, and throw together some semblance of a paper. Why some people work that way is the basis for arguments about psychology, but common sense should tell you such practices are deadly. As Sarah explains, "I did my first draft in two three-hour sessions—uninterrupted. No phone calls, no TV, no snack breaks. Just work. If I'm working on an idea and stop for a snack, then I have to rethink everything up to that point in order to continue. That wastes so much time!" And remember that Sarah works at a computer and types with flying fingers. Make your own comparisons. Get the point?

CHECKLIST FOR DRAFTING

When you finish your first draft, you should be able to answer "yes" to the following questions. Other questions about techniques introduced here will be included in the Checklist for Chapter 11, the chapter on the revision process.

1. If I wrote with pen and paper, did I write on every other line and only on one side of my paper?
2. If I wrote at the computer, did I set it for a double-spaced format?
3. Did I save everything—even apparently irrelevant note cards or early drafts?
4. Did I make a conscious effort in my introduction to attract reader interest?
5. Have I stated or implied my thesis statement in the introduction?
6. Do the paragraphs correspond to my outline?
7. Did I follow the organization established in my outline or my revised outline?
8. Does each paragraph include a stated or implied topic sentence?
9. Do tables and figures stand alone, and is the text clear without the tables or figures?
10. Did I consciously follow one of the techniques for concluding my paper?
11. Have I included accurate and complete temporary documentation?
12. Have I included quotation marks around a source's exact words?
13. Did I omit irrelevant material from note cards that really do not support any of my main ideas?

EXERCISES

Exercise A: Turning Notes into Text

Directions: The following 11 note cards provided Sarah with the material she needed to write the third and fourth paragraphs of her paper, which follow. Discuss how the notes became text. What generalizations can you make about note taking?

Definition
(30) 13

"There is no generic swamp. Rather there are acid swamps, cedar swamps, river swamps, bay swamps, blackgum swamps and cypress swamps. There are fens in Massachusetts, bogs in Maine, prairie potholes in the Dakotas and sea grass beds and mangrove forests in Florida."

Definition
(27) 264-265

In northwoods, wetlands can be
　marshes
　alder thickets (along waterways)
　bogs
　bog forests (black spruce and
　　　tamarack)
　swamp forests (white cedar and
　　　black ash w/ rich understory)

Definition
(14) 19

"Essentially wetlands require saturated soils and vegetation adapted to periodic inundation."

Definition

(13) 20

"Bottomland hardwood forests are wetland areas characterized by saturated and poorly drained soils and specific tree species."

Definition

(1) 8

"Wetlands that fill in may become sedgy tussock marshes or wet meadows and may eventually develop into swamps dominated by wetland trees and shrubs."

Definition

(9) 40

Most threatened: "scattered tracts of private property you might drive right past"

Definition   ① 3

General term "wetlands" refers to

— Muskegs "northern boggy area (that) may support trees"

In Britain: moors, heaths

Fen: grassy marsh

Definition   EPA "Wetland Types"

Wetlands are areas "where water covers the soil, or is present either at or near the surface of the soil all year or for varying periods of time during the year, including during the growing season."

Definition (variations)   ㉕ 13-14

- a meadow if mowed, lacks shrubs
- swamp "dominated by trees and shrubs"
- marsh - lacks "woody plants, but grasses, cattails, reeds, sedges... thrive"
- bog - no water runs in or out, also acidic

Definition   (1) 2

"saturated with water for indefinite
or prolonged periods of time"

Can be swamp, marsh, bog can
have grass, shrubs, trees

Definition

tidal or salt marshes   (1) 3
bogs w/ evergreen trees
(peat 20-40 feet deep)
All are wetlands.

Paragraphs three and four from Sarah's paper:

The terms categorizing wetlands, however, still do not completely define them. As one writer explains the problem,

> There is no generic swamp. Rather there are acid swamps, cedar swamps, river swamps, bay swamps, blackgum swamps, and cypress swamps. There are fens in Massachusetts, bogs in Maine, prairie potholes in the Dakotas and sea grass beds and mangrove forests in Florida. (Booth 13)

To further complicate the problem of clear definition, wetlands change, becoming marshes, wet meadows, eventually perhaps shrub- or tree-filled swamps (Parrish). In addition, size does not define. In fact, the most threatened wetlands are not the big or famous but "scattered tracts of private property you might drive right past" (Easterbrook 40).

The EPA, however, follows this general definition: Wetlands are areas "where water covers the soil, or is present either at or near the surface of the soil all year or for varying periods of time during the year, including during the growing season" ("Wetland Types"). To put it plainly, if the soil is wet enough often enough to affect the vegetation, the area is a wetland.

Exercise B: *Analyzing Introductions*

Directions: Using the model student papers in Chapter 14, discuss the following questions about the introductions.

1. What technique does Terry use to introduce his paper about Steinbeck's *The Grapes of Wrath*?

2. Is Terry's thesis statement stated or implied? Why do you think he handles the thesis statement this way?
3. If his is a paper of contrast, what is the purpose of the fourth sentence in Terry's introduction?
4. Does Terry's introduction attract reader attention? Why or why not?
5. Having read the introduction, what message do you as a reader expect Terry's paper to convey?
6. What techniques does Sarah use to introduce her paper about wetlands?
7. Is her thesis statement stated or implied? Why do you think she handles the thesis statement this way?
8. Sarah's introduction includes a three-word sentence. Does it create emphasis? Why or why not?
9. Does Sarah's introduction attract reader attention? Why or why not?
10. Having read the introduction, what message do you as a reader expect Sarah's paper to convey?

Exercise C: Analyzing Body Paragraphs

Directions: Answer the following questions based on what you know should occur in the body of a research paper.

1. How does the outline designate the body paragraphs of a research paper?
2. In what order can body paragraphs be arranged?
3. What determines the order in which body paragraphs are arranged?
4. How are topic sentences related to the thesis statement?
5. Where does a research writer find supporting details for his or her topic sentences?
6. What is the purpose of transitions? When does a writer use them?
7. Why is temporary documentation important in the body paragraphs of a first draft?
8. What often causes a beginning research writer to have a choppy paper?
9. What rule of thumb can you give for including tables and figures in the text of a research paper?
10. If the text of a paper must be clear without the tables or figures, why include them?

Exercise D: *Analyzing Conclusions*

Directions: Using the student model papers in Chapter 14, answer the following questions about conclusions.

1. What technique does Terry use to conclude his paper about Steinbeck's *The Grapes of Wrath*?
2. What, if any, connection does Terry's conclusion have to his introduction?
3. What techniques does Sarah use to conclude her paper about wetlands?
4. What, if any, connection does Sarah's conclusion have to her introduction?
5. Do you, as reader, feel a sense of completeness about Sarah's and Terry's concluding paragraphs? Why or why not?

Exercise E: *Analyzing Transitions*

Directions: Study the following paragraph from Terry's paper. Identify the words and phrases that function as transitions in the numbered sentences. Some sentences have one word or phrase, some have more than one, and some have none. List each transitional word or phrase, and then write an explanation of its purpose.

(1) Another key in surviving the Great Depression was family unity. (2) As my grandfather, James Owen Gish, stated in a personal interview, his family "was very close." (3) Whenever a crisis came to one of its members, the family would band together to face it. (4) Even a son coming home after a long day of planting was met with the welcome of his entire family. (5) The family that prayed together did, indeed, stay together; and the Gishes prayed very often. (6) The Joads, on the other hand, fell apart like their car. (7) As George Bluestone writes in a 1972 essay, although Ma Joad "protests savagely to the breakup of the family" (105), her protests do not stop Al, Connie, and Noah from leaving the fold. (8) Another nail is struck into the family coffin when Ma appears

to go "jackrabbit" (185) and even tells Pa to "drive on" (249) while she bumps along in the back of the car with Granma Joad's corpse. (9) Whether because of poverty or insanity, the Joads cannot attain the winning power of family togetherness possessed by the Gishes. (10) The cliché that blood is thicker than water must certainly be true, but in the Dust Bowl, blood satisfied no one's thirst.

11

Revising
the Draft

Every step in the process of writing a research paper comes with its own set of demands, and revising is yet another of those steps. Essential to your success as a writer, revision is far more than copying neatly in ink or producing a computer printer version of your first draft. So, what does the revision process entail? This chapter suggests a step-by-step approach toward successful revising.

CHECKING CONTENT

These specific steps will help you check the content of your paper:

1 *Put distance between you and your paper.* When you finish the first draft, put it away for about 48 hours to give yourself time to reflect. Even after you put away pen and paper or turn off the computer, your mind keeps working, and that subconscious mental activity helps you gain objectivity.

TECH TIP

If you wrote your first draft at the computer, you will be able to edit better reading a printed copy rather than reading from the screen. So print a copy now, before you move on to the next step.

2 *Read the paper quickly for thesis support.* As you read, ignore errors, choppy sentences, missing transitions. Read only for content. Does your paper do what your thesis statement says it will do?

CRITICAL THINKING HINT

Another way to analyze content is to ask yourself if the paper answers your research question. If so, it probably does what your thesis statement says it will do. After all, the thesis statement is the answer to your research question! For instance, Sarah's research question was, "What are the effects of destroying wetlands?" (See Chapter 2.) Her thesis statement answers, "When the earth's citizens recognize wetlands' values, perhaps they will be more concerned about the protection of those vanishing areas." (See Chapter 9.) She must read her paper to see that she shows her reader why wetlands must be protected.

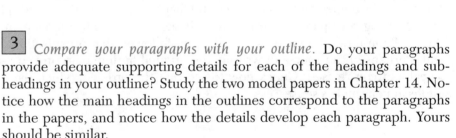

3 *Compare your paragraphs with your outline.* Do your paragraphs provide adequate supporting details for each of the headings and sub-headings in your outline? Study the two model papers in Chapter 14. Notice how the main headings in the outlines correspond to the paragraphs in the papers, and notice how the details develop each paragraph. Yours should be similar.

4 *Analyze the tone of your paper.* Do you maintain the same attitude throughout your paper? For instance, have you slipped into a flippant tone in one section while the remainder of the paper is critical? Is one section humorous while the rest is serious?

5 *Examine the paper for unity.* Be sure that every paragraph directly supports the thesis statement and that you have avoided including a paragraph or two simply because you have "interesting" note cards that do not fit anywhere else in your outline. Get rid of irrelevancies! For instance, Sarah found interesting material about legislation approving payment to farmers who allowed drained land to return to wetlands. Those details, however, did not support her thesis, so she did not put them in her paper.

6 *Check the length.* Your assignment for this research paper probably included some kind of reference to length, either in pages or words. (A printed page is about 250 words.) If your paper is too short, you will need to gather additional supporting details. Notice that we are talking about gathering more material, not "padding" your paper. Teachers are experts at seeing through such attempts, so wordiness gains nothing but criticism.

On the other hand, your paper may be too long. In that case, analyze your outline. Are there unnecessary supporting paragraphs? Have you included irrelevant material? Is your topic too broad? As you make cuts, be sure that you still support your thesis.

7 *Check for direct quotations.* Take a quick count. Have you limited direct quotations to no more than 20% of your paper? If not, paraphrase or summarize. Eliminate the quotations that lend no authority or emphasis to your paper. Be certain, however, to avoid plagiarism.

CHECKING ORGANIZATION

When you developed the final outline in Chapter 9, you chose a method for organizing your paper. Your outline reflected that organizational plan. The question now, of course, is whether you followed that organizational plan. Perhaps in the course of writing, the original outline plan proved illogical and you revised. Check now to see that the order in which paragraphs appear makes sense.

CRITICAL THINKING HINT

Can you defend the order in which your paragraphs appear? Can you give specific reasons why one paragraph should appear before or after another? To be unable to give such a defense and explanation suggests that you have not critically analyzed the organization of your paper. Do it now!

If you find flaws in your organization—or worse yet, find no organization at all—restructure your paper. Move paragraphs as necessary to arrange your main ideas logically. Simply cut your paper apart between paragraphs and then tape it back together in the revised order. Terry, for instance, found that by moving his first paragraph so that it appeared just before the conclusion, he strengthened his argument. By making this change, Terry first described obvious differences that were advantages and ended with a difference that should have been a disadvantage but was not. Thus, he created for his logical reader an even greater distinction between the two families.

TECH TIP

If you prepared your first draft at the computer, you can easily cut and paste to move a whole paragraph, try it in a new location, and move it back if you find the new order unsatisfactory.

CHECKING PARAGRAPH STRUCTURE

No magic formula exists for good paragraph structure. In general, however, each body paragraph should have the following:

1. an opening transitional word, phrase, or sentence connecting it to the previous paragraph
2. a topic sentence, stated or implied
3. adequate supporting details, including (but not limited to) examples, illustrations, statistics, anecdotes
4. transitional words and/or phrases showing the relationship among supporting details
5. usually, a concluding sentence or idea

See how the following paragraph from Terry's paper incorporates all the components of a good paragraph:

Another key in surviving the Great Depression was family unity. As my grandfather, James Owen Gish, stated in a personal interview, his family "was very close" (12/23/91). Whenever a crisis came to one of its members, the family would band together to face it. Even a son coming home after a long day of planting was met with the welcome of his entire family. The family that prayed together did, indeed, stay together, and the Gishes prayed very often. The Joads, on the other hand, fell apart like their car. As George Bluestone writes in a 1972 essay, although Ma Joad "protests savagely to the breakup of the family" (105), her protests do not stop Al, Connie, and Noah from leaving the fold. Another nail is struck into the family coffin when Ma appears to go "jackrabbit" (185) and even tells Pa to "drive on" (249) while she bumps along in the back of the car with Granma Joad's corpse. Whether because of poverty or insanity, the Joads cannot attain the winning power of family togetherness possessed by the Gishes. The cliché that blood is thicker than water must certainly be true, but in the Dust Bowl, blood satisfied no one's thirst.

Transition and topic sentence

First supporting idea

Example

Transition and next example

Summary of first set of details

Transition and second supporting idea

Example

Transition and second example

Conjunction and third example

Transition and logical conclusion from examples

Concluding statement

Inexperienced research writers chronically suffer from inadequate supporting details. A handwritten paragraph that takes half a page looks long but in reality may have only two or three sentences. While there is no magic number of sentences required for a successful paragraph, the odds are that such a brief paragraph lacks sufficient details. Sentences, however, do vary dramatically in both length and content. The final judgment lies with your reader.

CRITICAL THINKING HINT

At this point, the thought of returning to the library is almost noxious. Nevertheless, analyze your paragraphs carefully in terms of supporting details. Do you have sufficient examples, illustrations, or other details to fully support every topic sentence?

How do you know whether you need more supporting details? Become the objective reader. Put yourself in the place of your audience. Does your paper give enough detail for your audience to accept your idea?

Analyze your paragraphs with these two points in mind:

1. The more complicated the idea, the more support you need.
2. The more unfamiliar the idea to your readers, the more support you need.

If your analysis shows weakly supported paragraphs, swallow that sick feeling, return to the library, and gather the necessary additional details.

Finally, check both the introduction and conclusion. Try this method: read the introduction aloud, then immediately read the conclusion aloud. Do they show continuity? Does the conclusion reflect the ideas in the introduction? At the same time, does the conclusion avoid sounding like a rerun of the introduction? Refer again to Chapter 10 and review the guidelines for writing good introductions and conclusions.

CHECKING SENTENCE STRUCTURE

When you have the content in good shape, check for sentence structure. Read each sentence, compare it to the one preceding and the one following, and make any needed revisions. Use the following guidelines:

Accuracy in Sentence Structure

This text assumes you have a solid background in grammar, mechanics, and usage. Make sure you follow these general guidelines:

1. Avoid sentence fragments.
   Incorrect: Only some of George Washington's portraits clearly show his skin. Seriously scarred from smallpox.
   Correct: Only some of George Washington's portraits clearly show his skin seriously scarred from smallpox.

2. Eliminate run-on sentences and comma splices.
   Incorrect: People worry about endangered species like pandas, polar bears, and leopards, about 90% of now-extinct animals were birds.
   Correct: People worry about endangered species like pandas, polar bears, and leopards, but about 90% of now-extinct animals were birds.

3. Omit dangling or misplaced modifiers.
   Incorrect: After checking calendars, Will Rogers Day is a legal holiday only in Oklahoma.
   Correct: After checking calendars, researchers determined that Will Rogers Day is a legal holiday only in Oklahoma.

4. Delete redundancies.
   Incorrect: Tax forms, returned back to the government, reveal abundant personal information.
   Correct: Tax forms, returned to the government, reveal abundant personal information.

5. Delete wordiness.
   Weak: Tax forms reveal a great abundance of all kinds of personal information.
   Improved: Tax forms reveal abundant personal information.

6. Create parallel structure for coordinating parts.
   Incorrect: Cures for the black plague included releasing spiders in the house, people who were dying had warm bread

over their mouths, sitting between two fires, and when swallows were in the area they were killed.

Correct: Cures for the black plague included releasing spiders in the house, placing warm bread over the mouths of the dying, having the patient sit between two fires, and killing swallows.

7. Put main ideas in main clauses.

Weak: A person can use a formula that measures assets and liabilities to determine net worth.

Improved: A formula measuring assets and liabilities will determine net worth.

Variety in Sentence Lengths

Do a word count. Are most sentences the same length? If so, try to make some shorter and some longer (without committing serious grammatical errors). Figure the average sentence length either for your entire paper or for representative paragraphs. Very short averages suggest immature writing.

TECH TIP

Word processing programs include a word count tool. Using it will save the labor of word-by-word counting.

Some programs also include a style checker, either as part of the word processing program or as a separate piece of software. Style checkers will usually give not only a word count but also an analysis of reading level (i.e., the maturity of your writing).

Variety in Sentence Structure

Analyze the structure of each of your sentences to determine variety. By implementing a variety of sentence structures, you will submit a paper that shows maturity and reads well—never a detriment when you know your work will be evaluated!

CRITICAL THINKING HINT

In order to analyze sentence structure, use a chart. Let each mark symbolize one sentence in the designated paragraph. The following sample analysis represents the second paragraph from Terry's paper on *The Grapes of Wrath.*

Kinds of Sentences	Para. 1	Para. 2	Para. 3	Para. 4
Simple		///		
Simple/compound subject				
Simple/compound verb		/		
Compound		/		
Complex		////		
Complex/compound parts		///		
Compound-Complex				

No one is likely to have an equal number of each kind of sentence, but a heavy predominance of one kind suggests a need for revision.

In the complete analysis, strive for a variety of sentence types in the paper as a whole. Use a variety of ways of beginning sentences—with the subject, an introductory word or phrase, or perhaps an adverbial clause. Seek ways of combining sentences to express coordinating ideas—or contrasting ideas.

Then, as you make revisions, consciously generate emphasis. For instance, a three- or four-word sentence following one or two long ones catches attention and strikes a blow to the reader's inner ear. Study this example from a draft of Sarah's paper:

```
Because giant parking lots, acres of buildings, masses of concrete,

and many square miles of pavement literally waterproof the land,

rainwater cannot soak in; so it is concentrated in large runoffs.

Floods result.
```

The thirty-one-word compound-complex sentence is followed by a two-word whopper. The emphasis—the impact—is obvious.

To "hear" the impact your sentence structure will have on your reader's inner ear, read your paper aloud or ask someone else to read it to you. Listen for monotonous passages, dull rhythms, choppy sections. Rewrite until you hear music!

Accuracy in Word Choice

Finally, read sentences for precise word choice. Refer to a thesaurus if you find yourself using certain words repeatedly. On the other hand, avoid using the thesaurus merely to find "bigger" words. Bigger is not necessarily better, and is often worse.

TECH TIP

If your word processing software includes a thesaurus, use it to speed your search for precise words. Some programs include antonyms as well as synonyms and permit cross-references to other synonyms.

CHECKING MECHANICS, USAGE, AND STYLE

Again, this text assumes you have a solid background in mechanics and usage. Use the following to check for common errors:

1. Make subjects agree with their verbs.
   Incorrect: A bowl of oranges sit on the table.
   Correct: A bowl of oranges sits on the table.

2. Make pronouns agree with their antecedents.
   Incorrect: Everyone should spend their time wisely.
   Correct: Everyone should spend his (or her) time wisely.

3. Maintain consistent point of view, generally third-person.
   Incorrect: Most readers enjoy fiction, but if you prefer nonfiction, let me recommend a good book.
   Correct: Most readers enjoy fiction, but for those who prefer nonfiction, this is a good book.

4. Use present tense for comments by you and your sources.
   Incorrect: Easterbrook wrote; the research showed
   Correct: Easterbrook writes; the research shows

5. Use past tense to discuss events or concepts from the past.
   Incorrect: John Steinbeck lives
   Correct: John Steinbeck lived; the novel proved controversial during the 1940s

6. Follow the conventions for punctuation.
   Incorrect: Two residents both of whom registered complaints appeared at a press conference, no one seemed impressed by their concerns.
   Correct: Two residents, both of whom registered complaints, appeared at a press conference; no one seemed impressed by their concerns.

7. Wherever reasonable, avoid passive voice and weak linking verbs.
   Weak: Music videos are enjoyed by many teenagers.
   Improved: Many teenagers enjoy music videos.
   Weak: A great deal of time is spent by teachers marking papers.
   Improved: Teachers spend a great deal of time marking papers.

8. Wherever reasonable, avoid contractions.
   Informal: The new law won't solve all problems.
   Formal: The new law will not solve all problems.

Refer to a general English handbook if you have questions about grammar, usage, mechanics, and stylistic details.

TECH TIP

Two matters for your consideration:

1. Use the *search* or *find* commands to locate words you know you have misspelled or errors you know you sometimes make. For instance, you can ask the computer to find "you" to check for second-person point of view. You can also ask the computer to find "their" and "there" if you sometimes confuse the two. Ask the computer to find apostrophes if you want to check for contractions.

2. Some style checkers will spot omitted parentheses and quotation marks, locate grammatical errors, or note passive voice. Do not take style checkers too seriously, however, for most will misguide uninformed writers. For example, a style checker may show the reading level of a paper is 5 (i.e., fifth grade). An uninformed writer may then add big words or longer sentences to raise the reading level. This could muddy an otherwise clearly presented paper.

TIME MANAGEMENT GUIDELINES

Thorough revision takes time and is the mark of a good writer. Unfortunately, research papers are inevitably due on a specific date with appropriate penalties for tardiness. Use the following guidelines for the revision process so that you can complete the final draft on time:

Number of weeks until final paper is due	Number of days available for revising
10	4
8	3
6	3
4	2

TWO STUDENTS' PROGRESS

Acknowledging that writers differ in their working styles as much as in their personalities, this part of the chapter gives insight into two students' approaches to revision strategies.

Sarah

Since I tend to be pretty methodical, I thought I should work through the paper checking for only one problem at a time. In other words, I should read once just for organization and read again for sentence structure, and so on. But I didn't. Instead, I found myself working paragraph by paragraph.

Starting with the introduction, I analyzed content, paragraph structure, sentence forms, word choice, and mechanical problems—everything our teacher said we were supposed to check. I made revisions. Then I moved on to the next paragraph. Some people probably work differently, but that method suited me.

As you already know, I like to write at the keyboard, but I discovered that I caught different kinds of errors reading on-screen material as opposed to reading printed copy. As a result, I revised from both kinds of text. It seems that for me the little things showed up more in print and the other things—like goofy sentences—showed up more on screen. In spite of my preference for writing at the keyboard, I have to admit that text *does* look different on paper. It may sound silly, but we have to remember that our readers will see this stuff only on paper.

Because I kept fiddling with little things, I really didn't keep track of how many revisions I made, but I can tell you how many I printed out: five. The fifth was the final draft. Here's a sample of how just the introductory paragraph changed from first to final draft.

First Draft

[Sentences are numbered for ease in discussion; numbers were not, of course, included in either of Sarah's drafts.]

(1) Quaking bogs and snake-infested, mosquito-ridden swamps make up the stuff of chiller movies. (2) When the chase is on, the man on the run hides in the gooey, slimy swamp where no civilized human would go. (3) Ooze creeps up around ankles and shins, floundering the strongest runner. (4) Creepy crawly things inhabit the gloom. (5) With the longtime image of wetlands being one of revulsion, it is no wonder the battle to save them—or what's left of them—has been so difficult. (6) When society recognizes wetlands' values, however, support for their preservation will surely grow.

Final Draft

(1) Quaking bogs and snake-infested, mosquito-ridden swamps make up the essence of chiller movies where the gooey slime hides both crime and criminal, and the gloom is home to creepy crawly things. (2) These are wetlands. (3) Is it any wonder the battle to save them—or what's left of them—has been so difficult? (4) When the earth's citizens recognize wetlands' values, however, perhaps greater preservation measures will result.

Two interesting things happened during the revision process. First, the text tightened, so I actually reduced the length of some paragraphs. You can see that in the example. Second, I found that most revisions came as the result of working with sentence structure. The overall stuff was there—content and organization. The other things needed lots of attention!

Terry

I wrote my first draft with pen and paper, crossing out, inserting arrows, adding words and phrases and sometimes whole sentences between lines. When I thought I had made all the usual revisions, I entered a "final" draft into the computer. When I saw this supposedly final draft on screen and in print, I saw more needed changes. Seems like putting something in print makes me see shortcomings in my paper. Maybe it's the way our teacher explained it: when you see something in print, there's a subconscious expectation. You expect it to sound professional, look professional, *be* professional. When it isn't, well, that's when you need to revise.

Before I printed a copy, I thought my introduction sounded good. When I saw the text on screen and then off the printer, I knew it needed help. Notice the differences in these two introductory paragraphs.

[Sentences are numbered for ease in discussion.]

Early Draft

(1) In John Steinbeck's <u>The Grapes of Wrath</u>, the Joad family is driven from their home and forced to become nomads during the Great Depression. (2) On the other hand, my grandfather's family had no trouble holding onto their land during this time. (3) Through some means, my grandfather's family, the Gishes, felt less than a tremor of the economic quake that shook the fictional lives of the Joads.

Final Draft

(1) In John Steinbeck's <u>The Grapes of Wrath</u>, the difficulties of the Great Depression drove the Joad family from their home and forced them to become nomads. (2) On the other hand, my grandfather's family, the Gishes, had no trouble holding onto their land during this period of economic crisis. (3) In many respects, the two families shared common backgrounds. (4) Both families were from the South; both started out in the Depression as landowners; both had families with multiple children. (5) The Gishes and the Joads shared these three obvious similarities, yet due to their own strengths, the Gishes felt less than a tremor of the economic quake that shook the fictional lives of the Joads.

The printed version made me more conscious of the need for transitions, too. Our teacher told us to use transitions to tell readers that we're going on to another point. Additional transitions made my paper smoother.

TIPS AND TRAPS

Sarah gives her best advice: "Allow time between drafts, time for ideas to percolate through your subconscious." As she explains, "I needed to work through the whole paper several times. The time between drafts gave me the objectivity—the distance, if you will—to read my own paper as someone else might read it."

Terry adds, "Sarah's right, but I'd explain it a different way. You know, you write something a certain way because you think it's the right way to say it. Nobody writes down something he *knows* is wrong. That's why revising is so hard. You have to get away from yourself in order to be able to see a *need* for revising."

If there is a common weakness among student writers, it is that they do not do enough revision. Perhaps they do not understand how to revise; perhaps they lack motivation. Suffice it to say that students who are most successful learn to improve their work by reorganizing, restructuring, rephrasing, rewording. If you cannot see ways to revise, ask a classmate to read and offer suggestions. (But be careful whom you ask. Your best friend may be reluctant "to find anything wrong.")

CHECKLIST FOR REVISING

You should be able to answer "yes" to the following questions about your own revision process.

1. Do I do in my paper what the thesis statement says I will, i.e., answer the research question?

2. Do I have a defensible reason for arranging paragraphs in the order I do?

3. Did I follow my outline or its revision?

4. Have I maintained the same attitude throughout my paper?

5. Are all of my paragraphs well written?
   a. Does each have a topic sentence, stated or implied?
   b. Does each include enough supporting details to defend its topic?
   c. Does each paragraph maintain unity, i.e., does every detail included support the topic sentence?

d. Do transitional words, phrases, or sentences connect ideas within paragraphs?

e. Does each paragraph have a concluding idea or sentence (where needed)?

6. Do transitional words, phrases, or sentences connect ideas between paragraphs?

7. When I combine the topic sentences from each of the paragraphs, do they logically equal the thesis statement?

8. Have I written structurally accurate sentences, avoiding fragments, run-ons, comma splices, dangling and misplaced modifiers, and redundancies?

9. Have I used parallel structure for coordinating elements?

10. Have I varied my sentences by length?

11. Have I varied my sentences by structure?

12. Do my sentences create emphasis for important points?

13. Did I check for accurate word choice?

14. Did I check the grammar, mechanics, and usage?

EXERCISES

Exercise A: *Comparing Drafts*

Directions: Use the drafts of Sarah's and Terry's introductory paragraphs on pages 210 and 212 to discuss the following questions about the revision process.

Part 1: Sarah's Drafts

1. In what way does the new sentence 2 improve the final draft?

2. Why do you think Sarah combined sentences 1–4 in the first draft into one sentence in the final draft?

3. Explain how sentences 1–4 are combined to create one sentence.

4. Do you think the final sentence is better in the first draft or the final draft? Why?

5. The final draft is shorter than the first draft. Is the shorter length an improvement? Why or why not?

Part 2: Terry's Drafts

1. What change occurs in the first sentence from the early draft to the final draft? Is that an improvement? Why or why not?

2. In sentence 2, is "period of economic crisis" better than "time"? Why or why not?

3. Sentences 3 and 4 are added in the final draft. What purpose do they serve?

4. Compare the final sentence in each draft. Why do you think Terry made the change he did in the final draft?

5. The final draft is longer than the early draft. Do you think the added length improves the paragraph? Why or why not?

Exercise B: Analyzing Revisions

Directions: Study the changes made between the first and final drafts of this paragraph from Sarah's paper. Answer the questions that follow the revisions. Sentences have been numbered for easy reference.

First Draft

(1) Marine life is drastically affected by wetlands destruction. (2) "Two-thirds of fish and shellfish species taken along the Atlantic and Gulf Coasts and one-half of the Pacific Coast species rely on coastal wetlands for food, spawning, and/or nursery areas" (17–42). (3) To destroy those wetlands, then, is to take seafood off restaurant menus and grocery shelves ("Values").

Final Draft

(1) The effect of wetlands destruction on plant life tells only half the story. (2) The other half belongs to animal life,

beginning with marine creatures. (3) Of all of the fish and shellfish harvested commercially and privately from both east and west coasts, between one-half and two-thirds of the species rely on coastal wetlands for reproduction. (4) To destroy those wetlands, therefore, is to take seafood off restaurant menus and grocery shelves ("Values").

Questions

1. Sentence 1 in the first draft never appears in the second draft. Should it? Why or why not?

2. What purpose is served by the first two sentences in the second draft?

3. Sentence 2 in the first draft shows marked changes in the second draft (now sentence 3). What revisions have been made? Why do you think Sarah made those changes? Are any of these changes improvements? If so, what are they?

4. Are quotations used wisely in either or both drafts? Why or why not?

5. In the final sentence, "then" becomes "therefore." Why do you think Sarah changed that word? Is the second choice better than the first? Why or why not?

Exercise C: *Applying the Checklist*

Directions: Use the Checklist on pages 213–214 to evaluate your own paper. Respond in writing to each of the 14 items, explaining the changes you made and the questions you still have about additional revisions.

12

Preparing the Final Manuscript

The final manuscript of almost every research paper must be produced at the keyboard and printed. Specific rules govern everything about that printed copy—width of margins, spacing between lines, spacing for paragraph indentation, color of ink—everything. This chapter guides you through those regulations.

MANUSCRIPT FORM

Follow these rules for preparing the final manuscript of your research paper:

1. Use 8½" × 11" white paper. Print on only one side. Use twenty-pound bond paper for a neat appearance.
2. Always make a copy of your paper and keep it. The copy may be a photocopy or another printout.
3. Use a basic font. Avoid fancy fonts or colored ink.
4. Avoid dividing words at the ends of lines. Ragged right margins are expected, so make life easier for your reader by eliminating end-of-line hyphenations.

TECH TIP

Do *not* justify the right margins of a research paper.

Avoid using varied print fonts, such as for titles, unless your teacher agrees to such stylistic devices.

If your word processing software includes an automatic hyphenation feature, turn it off. You will have one less problem to check (especially since automatic hyphenations are sometimes incorrect).

5. Double-space the entire paper, including the Works Cited page and long quotations.
6. Use one-inch margins on all four sides of the paper.
7. Avoid widows and orphans, printer's terms for a single line (or word) of the text of a paragraph that appears at the bottom of a page (orphan) or top of a page (widow). Always have at least two lines of a paragraph at the end of a page break and at least one full line and part of another at the beginning of a page break.

TECH TIP

Your word processing software may permit you to override preprogrammed commands with one that automatically eliminates widows or orphans. If not, simply preview pages prior to printing and force page ends as necessary.

8. Research papers generally do not require a title page. Thus, certain identifying information appears on the first page of the text.
   a. At the right margin, a half inch from the top, enter your last name and the Arabic number 1. Do not write *page* or the abbreviation *p.*; write only the number. Do not use a comma between your name and the page number. This information, repeated on each consecutive page, is called the "running head."
   b. At the left margin, one inch from the top, on four double-spaced lines, enter your name, your teacher's name, the course title, and, in day/month/year order, the date the paper is due.

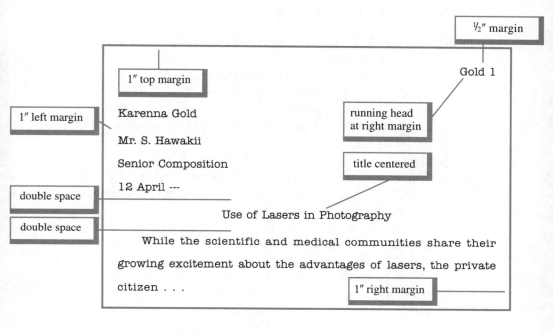

c. Continue to double-space after the date. Center the title. Do not underline or put quotation marks around the title. Use only initial uppercase letters but use initial lowercase letters for prepositions, articles, and coordinating conjunctions.

d. Continue to double-space after the title and begin your text. Indent five spaces for each paragraph.

9. On each page thereafter, enter your last name and page number in the upper right corner, a half inch from the top and one inch from the right margin. Number all pages consecutively.

TECH TIP

Word processing software has automatic numbering capability, so enter a command at the beginning of the file to run a header on every page at the flush-right margin. Most software will allow you to design a header that includes both your name and the page number. You will have no further work with pagination.

10. Begin text on all pages one inch from the top.

11. If you include a quotation that runs more than four printed lines, use the following format:
    a. Use a colon before a long quotation only if the text is an introduction to the quotation. Words like "the following," "as follows," or other phrases of similar meaning often indicate the need for a colon. If the quotation completes your own sentence, omit the colon.
    b. Begin the quotation on a new line.
    c. Enter the entire quotation indented ten spaces from the left margin. Maintain the one-inch right margin. Maintain double-spacing between lines.
    d. Do not use quotation marks either before or after the quotation. By setting off the lines, you have already clarified that the material is quoted.
    e. Place parenthetical documentation after the quotation, one space after the last mark of punctuation.
    f. Begin a new line to continue text. Do not indent five spaces unless the new line is also the beginning of a new paragraph.

12. If you have tables or figures, put them as close as possible to the text they support or illustrate. Follow these rules:
    a. Number each table or figure, beginning with 1. Beginning at the left margin, write "Table 1" or "Fig. 1" followed by a period.
    b. Skip two spaces and, on the same line as the table or figure number, type the title for the table or figure. Give titles for tables *above* the tabulated material; give titles for figures *below* the material.
    c. For words in the title, use initial uppercase letters except for prepositions, articles, and conjunctions.
    d. Document the source of tables or figures below the material. Use the same documentation form for tables and figures as you use for the rest of the paper.

13. If you quote poetry, quote up to three poetic lines by using quotation marks around the quoted work and separating the lines of poetry with the slash (/) mark. If you quote more than three lines, treat the poetry as a long quotation (see item 11) and maintain the poetic form.

14. Do not put your paper in a binder or folder unless your teacher instructs you to do so. Use a paper clip. Avoid staples or pins.

PARENTHETICAL DOCUMENTATION

The most common form of documentation is the parenthetical form. Previously, other forms of documentation—like footnotes and end-notes—have been preferable, but the advent of the computer has affected writers' working habits and ultimately the appearance of the final product. The models in Chapters 14 and 15 illustrate parenthetical documentation.

In your first draft (see Chapter 10), we suggested that you use a temporary documentation form involving two numbers: the first number represented the source and the second the specific page in that source. As you prepare your final manuscript, you must convert that temporary shorthand documentation into proper form. The number of the source must become a name, usually the author's name. Use these guidelines:

1. Place parenthetical documentation in the sentence where a pause would naturally occur: at the end of a sentence, at the end of a clause, at the end of a phrase.

2. After any quotation, paraphrase, or précis, enter a single space (as between words). Then, in parentheses, write the source name and the page number.
   a. Use the author's last name to indicate the source.

      Example: The stream waters flowing out of such wetlands are "cleaner than most municipally treated water" (Klockenbrink 72) and teem with fish, plants, and birds.

   b. If there are two authors, use both last names.

      Example: Annual wetlands productivity in Georgia's Alcovy River Swamp equals roughly a $3.1 million impact (Goodwin and Niering 4–7).

   c. If there is no author, use the title, shortened if possible. Use quotation marks or underscore as appropriate for the title.

      Example: Earlier labeled "the Rodney Dangerfield of the environment" ("Importance" 2), wetlands are gaining respect as an integral part of life's interdependence.

   d. If in your paper you use more than one work by a given author, you must identify both the author and the work. Separate the author's name from the title with a comma.

Example: "Since 1950 over 4.5 million acres of wetlands have been lost in the Mississippi flyway alone" (Kusler, "Roles" 43).

3. Do not use any punctuation between the name of the source and the page number. Place sentence-end punctuation immediately *after* the close parenthesis. Place close quotation marks *before* the open parenthesis.

Example: "Unless we take prompt action to preserve the native habitats, carnivorous plants will vanish in a few short years" (Bender 74).

4. If the author's name appears in the text of your paper, place only the page number in parentheses.

Example: In an editorial, Peter A. A. Berle wrote, "Economists still are not good at comparing the value of a wetlands ecosystem with that of a shopping-center parking lot . . ." (6).

5. If the quotation ends with an ellipsis, insert the parenthetical documentation after the close of the quotation marks but before the final period. (See example for guideline number 4.)

6. If you use indirect information, acknowledge the secondary source in the documentation. (If possible, of course, use the original source as well, for authenticity.)

Example: As Chief Seattle said in 1854, "Whatever happens to the beasts soon happens to man" (qtd. in Walter 40).

7. If a summary comes from several sources, all sources appear in a single parenthetical reference. Separate listed sources by semicolons.

Example: Farmers, environmentalists, and government agree that agriculture is to blame for 87% of recent wetland losses (Walter 28; "Saving Swamps" 44; Tiner 32).

8. In citing classic literary works, which are available in many editions, page numbers help only someone using the same edition you used (as identified in your Works Cited page). To help others, cite chapters, acts and scenes, lines, parts, cantos, etc.

Example: In <u>Hamlet</u>, the reference "to thine own self be true" (1.3.82) may be one approach to self love. [The parenthetical reference refers to Act I, Scene III, line 82. (Lines vary with editions.)]

WORKS CITED PAGE

The Works Cited page lists all sources—books, magazines, newspapers, electronic media, films, interviews, letters, maps, etc.—from which you have gathered information. It is an alphabetically arranged list of your bibliography cards and follows exactly the form you used for your cards.

Place the Works Cited page following the final page of your text and comply with these guidelines:

1. Enter the page number (the next consecutive number after the last page of text), like other page numbers in the text, a half inch from the top margin, flush with the right margin, preceded by your last name.

2. Center the title "Works Cited" one inch from the top of the page. Do not put quotation marks around the title or in any other way punctuate it. Use initial uppercase letters.

3. Continue double-spacing the entire page, both within and between entries.

4. Begin the first entry one double space below the title.

5. Begin all entries at the left margin, but indent subsequent lines five spaces (called "hanging indentation").

6. Adhere to the format for bibliography cards. (See model bibliography cards in Chapter 4 and model Works Cited pages in Chapter 14.)

7. Enter all sources in alphabetical order by the first word on your bibliography card: author's last name or title of article. If a title begins with *A, An,* or *The,* alphabetize by the next word.

8. Be sure that every parenthetical citation included in your text has a corresponding entry on the Works Cited page.

9. If you cite two or more sources by the same author, adhere to these rules:
   a. Give the author's name in only the first entry.
   b. Subsequent entries indicate the same author by beginning with three hyphens followed by a period.
   c. Arrange the publications in alphabetical order by title.

   Example: Steinhart, Peter. "No Net Loss." <u>Audubon</u> July 1990: 8–21.
   —. "Standing Room Only." <u>National Wildlife</u> April–May 1989: 46+.

10. Maintain a one-inch bottom margin.

11. Continue entries on additional pages as necessary, omitting the "Works Cited" title on further pages, beginning the text one inch from the top.

TIME MANAGEMENT GUIDELINES

The time required for the completion of a final draft depends in large part on two conditions: whether or not you completed your rough draft and subsequent revisions on computer and whether or not you are a fast keyboarder. If you are a hunt-and-peck typist, you will obviously need far more time than does someone who has prepared earlier drafts on computer and now needs only to adjust margins, enter a few details, and print a final copy.

The following time frame assumes you fall somewhere in between— that you are reasonably fast at the keyboard but that you must type your entire text. Adjust the time up or down according to your own capabilities.

Number of weeks until final paper is due	Number of days available to prepare final manuscript
10	6
8	5
6	4
4	3

TWO STUDENTS' PROGRESS

Sarah and Terry share their own experiences to help you prepare your own final manuscript.

Sarah

Since I worked through all drafts at the computer, I had only to polish the manuscript form. The whole process took a matter of hours. The biggest time consumer for me was preparing the Works Cited page, getting every comma, every period, every space, every capital letter just right.

Some of my classmates didn't fare as well. My best friend Amber doesn't type well. She spent night after night trying to format a decent-looking final manuscript. She didn't know much about the software she was using and tried to put running heads in by inserting the text at the top of each page. Then she'd discover a paragraph or sentence missing and that would cause the head to drop two or three lines into the text of the next page. She couldn't figure out how to turn off the right-margin justification. And she didn't know how to use the commands to get rid of widows and orphans, so she just inserted blank lines. Then she'd make some corrections, alter the pages, and end up with several blank lines in the middle of a page somewhere. If I thought the Works Cited page was tough, imagine what happened to Amber. It nearly drove her wild because she didn't know how to do hanging indentation. I guess it pays to be familiar with the software before you start a project like this!

Terry

I did my final manuscript on the computer, but everything up until then I had done with pen and paper. Since I'm fast at keyboarding, I entered the complete paper in one reasonably short evening. My best advice, though, is to plan to complete the final manuscript several days ahead to allow for problems and still meet the due date. Several of my friends have had bad experiences when they waited until the last minute. There's always the unexpected: the power goes off, the printer quits working, some technical problem causes you to lose a page—or the whole text. And almost everyone has some last-minute question about formatting or some peculiar bibliography form. Worse yet, you may discover that you don't know how to make the printer produce the right margins or create hanging indentations or print running heads. Then you find out you're out of paper. That's no picnic! So don't wait until the last minute to produce the final manuscript.

TIPS AND TRAPS

Most students seem to agree that Murphy's Law goes into full effect during the preparation of the final manuscript: *Anything that can go wrong will.* Assume that the same will be true for you and allow ample time for this final preparation. Remember that no matter how hard you have worked up to now, if the final manuscript is shoddy, your entire effort looks shoddy—and your grade will probably be the same! Prepare for the fact that computers and printers sometimes develop mechanical problems during the eleventh hour of a big project. Admit to the fact that the pressure is on and that stress increases the chance for error. Assume that you will run out of paper, toner, and patience. Allow time for all!

CHECKLIST FOR THE FINAL MANUSCRIPT

Use the following checklist to evaluate the form of your final manuscript. You should be able to answer "yes" to each of these questions.

1. Have I used a good quality 8½″ × 11″ white paper, printed on only one side?

2. Have I double-spaced the entire paper, including long quotations and the Works Cited page?

3. Did I maintain one-inch margins on all four sides of my paper?

4. Did I place text to avoid widows and orphans?

5. Did I format the first page of my text correctly to include my name, the teacher's or instructor's name, the course title, and the due date on separate lines at the left margin?

6. Have I correctly maintained a running head with page numbers flush with the right margin and a half inch down from the top margin, beginning on page 1?

7. Did I set off quotations more than four lines long?

8. Did I include documentation after every quotation, précis, or paraphrase?

9. Have I used the correct form and spacing for documentation and correct punctuation with parenthetical references?

10. Have I used ellipses correctly?

11. Have I followed the guidelines for including tables and figures in the text of my paper?

12. Is the Works Cited page formatted correctly with a running head, title, and hanging indentation for all entries?

13. Is the Works Cited list correctly alphabetized?

14. If I used more than one work by the same author, did I begin the entries that follow the first one with three hyphens followed by a period rather than with the author's name?

15. Did I make a copy?

EXERCISES

Exercise A: *Formatting the First Page*

Directions: Use the following information to prepare an accurately formatted first page of a research paper.

1. The paper is titled "Using Solar Energy to Fuel Transportation."

2. The author, a student in Mr. Boris Kuscuskio's English VIII class, is Roberto Magliano.

3. Roberto's paper is due May 18, this year.

4. The opening paragraph begins this way:

U.S. dependence on foreign oil, the pollution spewed out by coal-fired generators, and the earth's limited nonrenewable fossil fuels have led to a closer look at alternative power. According to historian Jack Smith, scientists have struggled for years to find inexpensive ways to convert free solar power for daily use. Heat for homes and water has been in use for a decade or so, but it doesn't affect the greatest of this society's polluters: the automobile. On the other hand, experimental electric cars, on drawing boards for nearly a quarter of a century, have so many disadvantages that even the most energy-conscious shy away. Can engineers overcome these disadvantages in the near future?

5. Assume that Roberto got his information from these fictional sources:
   a. The first sentence is general knowledge.
   b. The second sentence is from page 19 of "Solar Power: A Short History," an article by Jack Smith on pages 18–22 in the magazine *Solar Transport*, an issue published in July, last year.
   c. Information for the third sentence comes from two sources: The first clause is from an article titled "Solar Uses" published on page 8 of the *Rockford Times* newspaper on June 18, last year. The second main clause comes from page 78 of a book titled *New Wave Automobiles* by Roger Jones. It was published last year by New Publishing House in Miami, Florida.
   d. The fourth sentence is from another Roger Jones source, this time on page 75 of an article titled "Where We Are and Where We're Going—Solar Powered Cars," which appeared in the October issue of *Car Talk*, last year, on pages 73–77.
   e. The last sentence is Roberto's research question, which he uses instead of giving away his thesis statement.

Exercise B: Formatting the Works Cited Page

Directions: Use the information above to create a Works Cited page. Use correct formatting.

Exercise C: Applying the Checklist

Directions: Use the checklist on pages 226–227 to evaluate your own final manuscript. Refer to specific chapter sections if necessary.

Proofreading

13

Here it is: the final step before you turn in your research paper, your last chance to catch any errors that may distract your readers. You have in front of you your final manuscript—no doubt a veritable work of art! Lurking in there somewhere, though, may be some monster waiting to destroy the results of your weeks of work. Maybe instead of a monster, only a group of little trolls has crept in. In either case, you want them out! And remember, even if someone else keyboarded your text, only you are responsible for the final copy. Check it!

READING FOR GRAMMAR, MECHANICS, AND USAGE

Telling you how to proofread is like telling you how to swim. This book can explain the steps, but only your own practiced knowledge can keep you from sinking. To tell you to read for grammar, mechanics, and usage problems implies that you have the background to recognize the errors.

As you read, follow these general recommendations:

1 *Read slowly.* Some writers find that after having written several drafts, they "read" words that are not there. Phrases sound familiar—and therefore correct—after so many repetitions. Thus, errors can easily go undetected. Reading slowly will force you to look carefully. Try reading aloud to a friend or even to yourself.

TECH TIP

Proofread from the printed copy, not just from the screen. Errors are more easily detected on paper since most readers seem subconsciously to expect printed material to be perfect.

2 *Look for typing errors.* Watch for three common keyboarding errors:
   a. Transposed letters. It is easy to enter *deteroirate* instead of *deteriorate* and not catch the transposition on a quick reading. You know what the word is supposed to be—you wrote it!—so you may skip over such little details.
   b. Missing letters. Reading too quickly will keep you from seeing the error in *depresion*. Keyboarding errors count heavily against you, for they are almost always considered spelling errors.
   c. Wrong letters. Sometimes you might hit the wrong key and enter a word that is correct but doesn't fit the sentence. For instance, if you enter *amply* instead of *ample*, you have simply hit the *y* instead of the *e*, but the result is a usage error, substituting an adverb for an adjective. Bad news!

TECH TIP

You may find comfort in a computer spell checker. However, do not let a spell checker lull you into complacency. Remember that as long as a word is spelled correctly, a spell checker will not point out a wrong word. It does not know that you meant to enter *out* and instead entered *our*. Even with a spell checker, you still must read your paper carefully.

3 *Check spelling.* That you must check spelling should go without saying, but all too often writers decide a word "looks right" and fail to check a dictionary. Misspelled words insult your reader.

4 *Read for punctuation.* Three general bits of advice:
   a. Read carefully for accurate punctuation with compound and compound-complex sentences. Doing so will help you eliminate

accidental run-on sentences or comma splices. If you need to review the rules, check a handbook for both commas and semicolons.

b. Beware of the advice to "punctuate where you pause." That advice often leads writers to sprinkle in needless punctuation. Too much is as bad as not enough. Put in punctuation as the rules indicate: if there is no rule, don't punctuate.

c. Check relative placement of punctuation marks used along with quotation marks. Always put periods and commas inside quotation marks. Always put semicolons outside quotation marks. Put other marks of punctuation inside quotation marks only if they are part of the quotation.

5 *Check for common grammatical errors.* The most frequent grammatical errors involve subject-verb agreement and pronoun-antecedent agreement. Read slowly to check for common errors.

Word processing software usually includes a tool for pointing out possible grammatical or stylistic errors. Be aware, however, that these so-called style checkers are not foolproof and can, in fact, cause the unwary writer to make changes for the worse. The best indication of their weakness is that no two will give you the same response about a given piece of writing. (Most even give the Gettysburg Address a poor evaluation.) So be alert. Grammar and style checkers are best suited to writers who already know the rules for grammar and usage and understand how to use them—and when to break them. In those instances the programs can help writers make sound decisions about possible changes.

6 *Check for consistent point of view.* In most cases, the research paper should be written in third-person point of view. If the assignment demands a personal response, first-person point of view may be acceptable. Generally, avoid second-person point of view. For example:

Third person: The *author* presents *her* material.
Second person: *You* may be confused by the characters' names.
First person: The theme seems to *me* to deal with fate.

Your teacher or instructor may have specific requirements regarding point of view. Ask. Most important, maintain a consistent point of view.

7 *Check for consistent verb tense.* Inconsistencies in verb tenses cause reader confusion. Verbs show relationships in time; therefore, while simple past tense shows "yesterday," the more distant past must be represented by some perfect tense. The use of tense is often confused in literary papers since the literary work continues to exist and is, therefore, described in present tense.

> Example: Steinbeck's *The Grapes of Wrath* is set during the Great Depression and describes one family's struggle with economic crisis. (present tense)

The author, however, has finished the work, so references to authorship are in past or some form of perfect tense.

> Example: Steinbeck wrote the protest novel after having lived with migrant families, riding with them to California, where he wrote articles about his experiences for the *San Francisco News*. (past tense)

See other examples and explanations in Chapter 11, pages 207–208.

8 *Eliminate contractions, slang, and colloquialisms.* Most research papers are written in a rather formal (but not stuffy) style. Check for appropriate vocabulary.

CHECKING DOCUMENTATION

1 *Read the Works Cited page for mechanical errors.* Read the Works Cited page letter by letter, mark by mark. This page (or pages) requires your understanding of dozens of rules that govern such things as the use of uppercase and lowercase letters in names and titles, commas and periods in just the right places, dates in day/month/year order, quotation marks and colons in relationship to other punctuation—an almost endless array of details. For example, every entry must end with a period, and with only a few exceptions, every entry should have something underlined (or italicized). Check carefully.

2 *Check the Works Cited page for accurate alphabetization.* See Chapter 12 for a review of the techniques for alphabetizing entries.

3 *Check direct quotations.* Check note cards to make sure nothing has been altered or lost in the process of recopying drafts or in typing the final manuscript. You can easily lose track of a pair of quotation marks in the process of writing and rewriting your drafts. Check too that you put in the ending quotation marks as well as the beginning marks for every quotation. Because you are concentrating on documentation at the end of a quotation, you can easily forget the final quotation marks.

4 *Check for accurate documentation.* Are authors' names and sources spelled correctly? Are the page numbers accurate? Does the information correspond with what you originally wrote on your note cards?

5 *Check parenthetical notes against the* Works Cited *page.* Is every note represented on the Works Cited page? Are page references and spelling consistent? Are all sources listed on the Works Cited page actually cited in your text?

MAKING CORRECTIONS

Generally, research papers should be submitted without visible corrections. That may mean reprinting a page or more. Sometimes, however, a writer may notice an error when time will not permit correcting at the keyboard and reprinting. In that case, use black ink to make a neat correction. If you must insert a word or letter, use the caret ($\wedge$) to indicate the insertion. Do not expect to be applauded for manuscript appearance in this case, but a neat correction is always better than an error.

The computer permits you to make last-minute revisions and produce a new page within seconds. Even if your revisions are such that you must consequently reproduce the complete document, corrections are worth the extra minutes. Good impressions do make a difference.

TIME MANAGEMENT GUIDELINES

Proofreading is a final check for details, so you should plan to spend at least two hours, preferably uninterrupted, following the suggestions above. Longer papers may require several hours, but you should allow a day for this final process. After all, if you find an error, you must correct it; some errors may require retyping a page or more.

Number of weeks until final paper is due	Number of days available for proofreading and correcting
10	1
8	1
6	1
4	1

TWO STUDENTS' PROGRESS

Some advice from Sarah and Terry may help you in your own proofreading. Each uses his or her own technique to proofread carefully.

Sarah

Proofreading always seems so tedious. By the time I'm ready to proofread, I've practically memorized my paper. Of course, that makes objectivity nearly impossible. Our teacher, though, divided our class into "editorial groups" of four. As such, each of us had three objective readers who could read our papers with fresh eyes. [The teacher used the checklist on pages 235–236 to guide students' editorial efforts.] I was surprised at how many silly little things I had overlooked—all of them obvious as soon as someone else pointed them out: a couple of typing errors, a missing close quotation mark, an incorrectly capitalized title on the Works Cited page. Hooray for my peer editors!

Terry

My best advice is to read your paper aloud. So my family wouldn't think I'd gone bonkers, I went in my room, shut the door, and read "aloud to myself" as I call it. I found I'd omitted the second *s* in *Depression* about half the time I used the word. Until this slow reading, though, I had simply skipped over that typing error. I "saw" the word correctly because I knew what it was supposed to be. You really have to look at every letter. In a quick reading, *work* looks very much like *word*; *out* looks like *our*; *in* instead of *on* can slip past; *muck* can be read as *much*. And so on and on! I know you're probably sick of reading the paper by now, but—hey! one last time—

it's worth the effort to find those errors that can really detract from your final paper (and grade).

Of course, I found other minor errors, too. Fortunately, I had all my work saved, so all I had to do was open the file, make the changes, and zip out another copy. Just imagine how much time I would have needed to retype whole sections. Make your plans accordingly!

TIPS AND TRAPS

Far too many students slight—or even ignore—this crucial step in the process of writing. Whether you take Sarah's or Terry's or some other approach to proofreading, devote whatever time is necessary to give the final polish to your work. You have already spent weeks on the project. To show indifference now is nothing short of foolhardy.

CHECKLIST FOR PROOFREADING

You should be able to answer an honest "yes" to each of the following questions.

1. Have I looked carefully at every word, checking for keyboarding errors or misspellings?

2. Have I avoided dividing words at the ends of lines?

3. Is my punctuation accurate?

4. Did I check for grammatical errors, especially errors that I know I have made in the past?

5. Have I used a consistent point of view, probably third-person point of view?

6. Have I used consistent verb tenses?

7. Did I use correct manuscript style throughout the text? (Refer to the Checklist for the Final Manuscript on pages 226–227.)

8. Is the Works Cited page accurate as follows:
   a. Are the title and running head accurate?
   b. Are names spelled correctly?

c. Have I capitalized accurately?

d. Are punctuation marks correct, especially in relationship to other punctuation?

e. Does each entry end with a period?

f. Have I underlined (or italicized) and used quotation marks accurately?

g. Is the list of entries correctly alphabetized?

h. Have I correctly cited multiple works by the same author?

9. Did I check direct quotations to make sure they are accurate?

10. Did I check my text against my note cards to make sure I used necessary quotation marks, thus avoiding plagiarism?

11. Is my documentation accurate, with names spelled correctly and page numbers correct?

12. Are all sources cited in my paper also listed on the Works Cited page?

13. Are only sources cited in my paper included on the Works Cited page?

14. Does the paper reflect my best effort?

EXERCISES

Exercise A: *Practicing Proofreading*

Directions: The following paragraphs are from the body of Kevin's research paper on the coal industry and the hazards that above-ground miners face. This section details hazards from severe weather conditions. The paragraphs include the kinds of errors you should correct during the proofreading process. Proofread and make corrections.

Severy cold effects mining operations the same way it effects everyone, but on a much greater scale. Frozen ground cannot be reclaimed, so operations were seriously slowed. Hydraulic-systems become so sluggish that even with 180 tons of coal bearing down on the unloading doors, they won't open and the coal can't be unloaded (Lannon, 43). Sometines the coal freezes in the trucks or on the conveyor lines in the preparation plant. Pick axes swing to brake up the masses, such work also seriously slowed operations. (Jansen 17)

While severe cold hampered operations, rain is really the biggest problem. The pits may fill with water and have to be pumbed out. The haulroads become soupy paths with muck several feet thick; a nasty, sticky muck that drys to boots like concreet (Lannon p. 47) Even bulldozers get stuck. And getting a loaded 180-ton truck out of a pit may require a bulldozer behind pushing, while the brute power of the truck engine struggles to make the incline (Dukes 11)

Even wind can be trecherous. If the cables need repairing, on the 330′ boom of the dragline, someone must climb it to make the repairs—even if the winds reach 40 mph. (Follistein 7).

Exercise B: *Applying the Checklist*

Directions: Use the Checklist for Proofreading to analyze your own paper. Make final corrections as necessary.

14

Analyzing Two Humanities- Style Models

Two complete model research papers follow. Sarah's paper on the wetlands issue represents a social issues paper and is developed by cause and effect. Terry's paper on John Steinbeck's *The Grapes of Wrath* represents a literary paper and is developed by comparison and contrast. Both include primary as well as secondary research.

You have heard from Sarah and Terry throughout this text as they shared their frustrations and advice and the lessons they learned from experience. Now study their papers and the accompanying analytical comments. (Their outlines appeared on pages 168 and 169). These final pages will help you polish your own paper.

Blaser 1

Sarah Blaser

Ms. S. J. Wolf

Senior English

20 May ---

Wetlands: Of What Value?

Quaking bogs and snake-infested, mosquito-ridden swamps make up the essence of chiller movies where the gooey slime hides both crime and criminal, and the gloom is home to creepy crawly things. These are wetlands. Is it any wonder that the battle to save them—or what is left of them—has been so difficult? When Earth's citizens recognize wetlands' value, however, perhaps greater preservation measures will result.

At long last, wetlands are gaining respect as an integral part of life's interdependence. Part of the problem, however, of protecting wetlands is finding a definition everyone accepts. The federally accepted standard was developed in 1979 by L. M. Cowardin and three colleagues (31), who list five kinds of wetlands: marine (formed by ocean tides), estuarine (formed by salt water meeting fresh), lacustrine (formed by lakes), riverine (formed along rivers and streams), and palustrine (formed as marshes, swamps, and bogs). The current Environmental Protection Agency (EPA) Web site designates four types: marshes, swamps, bogs, and fens, with multiple subdivisions of each ("Values").

The terms categorizing wetlands, however, still do not completely define them. As one writer explains the problem,

> There is no generic swamp. Rather there are acid swamps,
> cedar swamps, river swamps, bay swamps, blackgum
> swamps and cypress swamps. There are fens in

Annotations (right margin):

- Running head, 1/2″ from top
- Student, teacher, and class identification, 1″ from top
- Date due, day/month/year
- Title, centered; colon separates title from subtitle
- Introductory paragraph; concludes with thesis statement
- Topic sentence
- Author name included in text; page follows
- Parenthetical explanation of terms
- Source cited in text; Web site has no page available
- Single-word transition
- Topic sentence
- Long quotation set apart from text

Blaser 2

Massachusetts, bogs in Maine, prairie potholes in the
Dakotas and sea grass beds and mangrove forests in
Florida. (Booth 13)

To further complicate the problem of clear definition, wetlands
change, becoming marshes, wet meadows, eventually perhaps shrub-
or tree-filled swamps (Parrish). In addition, size does not define a
wetland. In fact, the most threatened wetlands are not big or
famous or maybe not even obvious, but instead are "scattered tracts
of private property you might drive right past" (Easterbrook 40).

The EPA, however, follows this general definition: Wetlands are
areas "where water covers the soil, or is present either at or near
the surface of the soil all year or for varying periods of time during
the year, including during the growing season" ("Wetland Types").
To put it plainly, if the soil is wet enough often enough to affect the
vegetation, the area is a wetland.

Depending on how one defines wetlands and depending on
whose statistics one reads, anywhere from half to two-thirds of
the United States' wetlands have been destroyed. In 1987 only
99 million acres remained, an area about the size of California, less
than half of the original wetland acreage. Most authorities agree
that the United States is losing 400,000 to 500,000 acres of
wetlands a year (Dahl 3). For instance, wetlands once covered 25%
of Indiana; now the acreage is less than 4% (Ind. DNR).

The grievous losses are attributed to a number of factors. The
National Wildlife Federation attributes 54% of loss to agriculture and
46% to development, including the following human activities that
adversely affect wetlands: drainage, dredging and stream
channelization, dumping fill material, diking and damming, grazing,

Annotations (right margin):

- Documentation for long quotation following punctuation mark
- Transition
- No page number necessary
- Transitions
- Quotation woven into writer's own sentence
- Quotation for authenticity
- Source cited; no page available
- Paraphrase of previous quotation for clarity
- Words and numerals for large numbers
- List summarizes source's information

Blaser 3

tilling for crop production, building levees, logging, mining, introducing nonnative species, construction, and polluted runoff ("Threats"). As long as humans continue these detrimental activities, wetlands will continue to disappear.

Given these vast losses, the real question for many is why should anyone care, especially when wetlands are "reviled as mosquito havens" (Youth). As biological entities, however, wetlands improve water quality (acting as purifiers), recharge groundwater and reduce flooding (acting to retain water), and serve as habitat for half of the endangered and threatened species in the United States. They also contribute to biodiversity, fish and waterfowl habitat, and recreation (Ducks). Consequently, to destroy wetlands is to destroy a resource for plants and animals from the bottom of the food chain all the way up to humans.

Exploring the destruction of that resource leads first to the wide variety of plant life supported by wetlands: cattails, water hyacinths, reeds, rushes, shrubs, bushes, and, surprisingly, trees. In fact, many wetlands originally supported massive timber growth. While the loss of that harvested timber is easily identified, the loss of other plant life will not be so obvious. For instance, probably the most unusual wetlands are the small, inconspicuous carnivores that, like every other form of life on this planet, play a role in the overall ecological scheme. Their destruction ultimately affects the balance of nature (Youth).

The effect of wetlands destruction on plant life tells only half the story. The other half belongs to animal life, beginning with marine creatures. Of all of the fish and shellfish harvested commercially and privately from both east and west coasts, between

Conclusion for causes of destruction

Transitional paragraph; moves from causes to effects

Introduces next point; begins discussion of effects

Colon introduces list

Transitional phrase

Transitional clause

Transitional sentence

Blaser 4

one-half and two-thirds of the species rely on coastal wetlands for reproduction. To destroy those wetlands, therefore, is to take seafood off restaurant menus and grocery shelves ("Values").

> Parallel infinitive phrases for clear cause-effect relationship

The situation is just as serious for waterfowl. After the destruction of 90% of the 94,000 acres of wetlands in Nebraska's Rainwater basin, migrating waterfowl were so crowded that 80,000 birds died there of avian cholera in 1980 (Baldwin 27). While research focuses on waterfowl (because hunting licenses help finance the research), hundreds of thousands of other birds are affected in similar ways.

> Topic sentence with transitional phrase; continues discussion of effects

> Parenthetical explanation

In terms of wildlife in general, Gregg Easterbrook points out that while the public pays attention to endangered species like pandas and grizzlies, they ignore the "germline," a word he coined to refer to "the general genetic heritage, especially of lesser organisms that form the majority" (41) of other organisms. The germline, most likely found in swamps, should concern earth citizens even more than the individual endangered species, for whatever happens to animals soon happens to humankind.

> Author cited in text; need only page number

Wetlands, however, do more than protect living plants and animals. They also store water and then release it slowly, reducing the impact of floods and drought, a function some authorities claim is worth $1.78 trillion to Earth's citizens ("How Much"). Because giant parking lots, acres of buildings, masses of concrete, and many square miles of pavement literally waterproof the land, rainwater cannot soak in, so it is concentrated in large runoffs. Floods result. On the other hand, a one-acre swamp with only a foot of water will retain 330,000 gallons. Thus, every time a wetland is destroyed, the

> Transitional phrase

> Single-word transition

Blaser 5

environment is dealt a double blow. First, the area's underground water supply diminishes; second, area runoff increases, thereby escalating downstream flooding (Goodwin and Niering 7). As wetlands biologist Keith Poole emphasized in a personal interview, "We all live downstream."

| Transitional pair to clarify effects

| Complete in-text reference; no parenthetical citation needed

The loss of wetlands also results in the loss of nature's filtering system. Wetlands can remove sediments and pollutants like giant kidneys, a natural service some scientists value at upward of $1.70 trillion ("How Much"). They sponge up the pollutants such as heavy metals and agricultural runoff, consequently preventing these toxic materials from flowing into fragile estuaries and bays. In fact, wetlands can even filter sewage. The natural vegetation of a marsh, like cattails and bulrushes, creates a natural filter. Then algae feed on whatever particles are left while grasses function as a filter for the clean water (Lorion 1). In reality, wetlands are so effective at cleaning water that nearly 150 communities, including San Diego and Disney World, use artificial wetlands instead of traditional sewage treatment plants. In so doing, they reap a 50% to 90% savings while creating wildlife refuges at the same time. The stream waters flowing out of such wetlands are cleaner than most municipally treated water and teem with fish, plants, and birds ("Wetlands Clean"). To destroy wetlands, then, is to remove nature's kidneys. As Poole explained, "If you drink water, you suffer" when wetlands are lost.

| Topic sentence with transition; emphasizes effects

| Transition emphasizing effects

| General explanation

| Application to give impact to explanation above

| Personal interview needs no further documentation; refers to paragraph introduction

| Transition to conclude discussion of effects

Finally, wetlands also help maintain biospheric stability. Most important in the contribution to what circles Earth is the wetlands' role in producing oxygen (Niering 31–35). Scientific calculations

Blaser 6

indicate that "512 acres [of wetlands] produce a net increase of

twenty tons of oxygen per day" (Goodwin and Niering 5). That is no

small impact in a world that justifiably worries about the

greenhouse effect and the ozone layer.

The real problem, of course, is putting all these benefits in

terms of dollars and cents. According to most authorities, wetlands

are far more productive than any other ecosystem. On the other

hand, many scientists think the world cannot put a dollar value on

wetlands. David Ehrenfeld, a conservation biologist at Rutgers

University, points out that

> Fresh water is provided by a complex interaction of
>
> wetlands that filter water, forests and grasslands that store
>
> it, and rivers and lakes that supply it. Without fresh water,
>
> humans and all animals would die. In that sense, the value
>
> of nature cannot be measured. ("Should Nature")

In spite of the many indicators of wetlands' values, not

everyone is willing to see the benefits. In many communities,

property owners believe protecting wetlands stifles economic

development, but according to Robin Lesher, an ecologist with the

United States Forest Service, "We have to recognize that [wetlands]

are amenities to the community and not obstacles to development.

They contribute to the quality of life" (qtd. in Thompson). As with

any issue, both sides express valid concerns. Many Earth citizens,

though, are working toward retaining what precious few wetlands

remain. Even farmers who once drained wetlands as a routine

practice now recognize wetlands' value (Fullerton 28).

Annotations (right margin):

- Writer adds identifying phrase
- Transitional sentence
- Name and identification to add strength to quotation
- Admission of controversy
- Quoted in newspaper article, so name and identification important for credibility
- Refers back to earlier statement that 54% of wetlands' loss due to agriculture

Blaser 7

Many Earth citizens have joined dozens of organizations, action groups, and research societies that have as their goal to provide the finances, information, and laws to protect wetlands (Wolf-Armstrong). Nevertheless, ignorance remains the number one problem. In fact, wetlands losses often occur when someone fills land that simply wasn't wet enough for anyone to recognize as a wetland (Fullerton 28). Shouldn't federal and state laws protect such lands? As one critic lamented, "At best, existing wetland laws and programs only show the rate of loss" (Baldwin 18) because they are hard to understand and harder still to enforce.

Many people are beginning to overcome the chiller-movie image of wetlands and to understand the importance of wetlands as protectors. As Poole explained, "A hundred years ago we could float down a river, drink the water, and eat the fish without a second thought. Not anymore. But if we can reclaim the wetlands, we can clean up the rivers. And if we don't there will be nothing left for our children." If wetlands disappear, the cost, both direct and indirect, is not just in the billions of dollars, it is beyond measure.

[Margin notes:]

Quotation run in with text

References to introduction; reference to first part of paper

Quotation to add meaning to "importance"

Reference to final part of paper; leaves reader with serious thought

Blaser 8

Works Cited

Booth, William. "Rebuilding Wetlands: Nature Proves a Tough Act

　to Follow." The Washington Post 30 Jan. 1990: C13–14.

Cowardin, L. M., V. Carter, F. C. Golet, and E. T. LaRoe.

　Classification of Wetlands and Deepwater Habitats of the United

　States. Washington, D.C.: US Fish and Wildlife Service, 1979.

Dahl, Thomas E. "Status and Trends of Wetlands in the

　Conterminous United States." National Wetlands Inventory.

　2000. United States Fish and Wildlife Service. 23 Apr. 2004

　<http://wetlands.fws.gov/statusandtrends.htm>.

Easterbrook, Gregg. "Cleaning Up." Newsweek 24 July 1989: 26,

　42. Academic Search Elite. EBSCOhost. Evansville Public Lib.

　23 Apr. 2004 <http://www.evpl.org>.

Fullerton, Jane. "Wetlands Redefined Again." Farm Journal Mar.

　2003: 127: 28. MasterFILE Premier. EBSCOhost. West Terrace

　High School Lib., 22 Apr. 2004 <http://www.westterracehs.org>.

Goodwin, Richard H., and William A. Niering. Inland Wetlands of

　the United States: Evaluated as Potential Registered Natural

　Landmarks. Washington, D.C.: GPO, 1975.

"How Much Money Is Nature Worth?" Today's Science on File.

　Aug. 1997. Facts.com. EBSCOhost. Evansville Public Lib. 28

　Apr. 2004 <http://www.evpl.org>.

Indiana Department of Natural Resources Education Center. "Wade

　into a Wetland Workshop." E-mail to author. 10 Feb. 2004.

Niering, William A. Wetlands: The Audubon Society Nature

　Guides. New York: Alfred A. Knopf, 1985.

Title 1″ from top;
double space to
first entry

Hanging
indentation

Government Web
site including
signed Web page

Magazine accessed
on ASE database
through EBSCO
subscription service

Subscription service
accessed through
school library site

Book with
two authors

Blaser 9

Parrish, Fred K. "Marsh." <u>Encyclopedia Americana</u>. 2004. <u>Grolier</u>

<u>Online</u>. EBSCOhost. Evansville Public Lib. 15 May 2004

<http://go.grolier.com/>.

> Online encyclopedia reference

Poole, Keith. Personal interview. 29 Apr. 2004.

"Should Nature Have a Price?" <u>Today's Science on File</u>. Aug.

1997. <u>Facts.com</u>. EBSCOhost. West Terrace High School Lib.

28 Apr. 2004 <http://www.westterracehs.org>.

> Newspaper article accessed through database

Thompson, Lynn. "Cities Weigh Balance of Nature." <u>The</u>

<u>Seattle Times</u> 25 Feb. 2004: H10. NewsBank Info. EBSCOhost.

West Terrace High School Lib. 28 Apr. 2004 <http://

www.westterracehs.org>.

> Date of publication and date of access

"Threats to Wetlands." <u>National Wildlife Federation</u>. 2003.

National Wildlife Federation. 18 Apr. 2004 <http://nwf.org/

wetlands/threats.html>.

> Web site name same as Web site sponsor

"Values and Functions of Wetlands." <u>Wetlands</u>. 17 Jan. 2003.

United States Environmental Protection Agency. 28 Apr. 2004

<http://www.epa.gov/owow/wetlands/vital/what.html>.

"Wetland Functions." <u>Conservation</u>. Ducks Unlimited, Inc. 2002. 18

Apr. 2004 <http://www.ducks.org/conservation/

wetland_functions.asp>.

> Two pages from same Web site

"Wetlands Clean Sewage the Natural Way." <u>Today's Science on</u>

<u>File</u>. Oct. 1993. <u>Facts.com</u>. EBSCOhost. Evansville Public Lib.

28 Apr. 2004 <http://www.evpl.org>.

"Wetland Types." <u>Wetlands</u>. 24 Feb. 2003. United States

Environmental Protection Agency. 28 Apr. 2004

<http://www.epa.gov/owow/wetlands/types/>.

> Web page title followed by Web site followed by Web site sponsor

Wolf-Armstrong, Mark. "President's Message." <u>Restore America's</u>

> <u>Estuaries</u>. 2002. 28 Apr. 2004 <http://www.estuaries.org/

> presidentmessage.php>.

Youth, Howard. "Winged Messengers: Does Habitat Loss Signal

> Biodiversity's Death Knell?" <u>USA Today Magazine</u> Nov. 2003.

> <u>MasterFILE Premier.</u> EBSCOhost. Evansville Public Lib. 28

> Apr. 2004 <www.evpl.org>.

Gish 1

Terry Gish

Ms. Shirley Everett

20 January ---

Winners and Losers

In John Steinbeck's <u>The Grapes of Wrath</u>, the difficulties of
the Great Depression drove the Joad family from their home and
forced them to become nomads. On the other hand, the Gish
family had no trouble holding onto their land during this period of
economic crisis. In many respects, the two families shared
common backgrounds. Both families were from the South; both
started out in the Depression as landowners; both had families
with multiple children. The Gishes and the Joads shared these
three obvious similarities, yet due to their own strengths, the
Gishes felt less than a tremor of the economic quake that shook
the fictional lives of the Joads.

Piety is often one of the strongest life preservers in the sea
of despair, even in the financial despair of the Great Depression.
Strong religious beliefs, something the Joads lacked, pulled the
Gish family through tough times. <u>The Grapes of Wrath</u> character
Casey, an unofficial member of the Joad family, moves from
preaching about God to criticizing Him. Even though he is a
former servant of God, Casey ultimately professes that he does
not "know nobody named Jesus" (24) and says his "heart ain't
in it" (24) anymore. On the contrary, the Gish family marched
ceremoniously into church every Sunday and sat in the pews
with straight backs and wide eyes. The church was small and

Annotations (right margin):

- Introductory statement; refers to literary work
- Sets up comparison/contrast of thesis
- Establishes similarities in order to emphasize differences
- Thesis statement
- First topic sentence
- Gives details from literature
- Identifies page number in novel on which quotation found
- Transitional phrase; begins contrast

Gish 2

could not hold a great many people, but it did hold a great deal of love for God. The poverty of the outside world was forgotten when the wealth of heaven was at hand. Under the circumstances, however, perhaps the Joads should not be compared to the Gishes. It is impossibly difficult to thank God for food when there is none. It is hard to pray for more good health when nothing but sickness and death loom. The Gishes' fortune was that they had the will and the opportunity to believe in their religion. The Joads, on a sadder note, lived in a world where God and heaven were for the rich, and the poor knew only hell.

Another key in surviving the Great Depression was family unity. As James Owen Gish stated in a personal interview, his family "was very close" (12/23/91). Whenever a crisis came to one of its members, the family would band together to face it. Even a son coming home after a long day of planting was met with the welcome of his entire family. The family that prayed together did, indeed, stay together, and the Gishes prayed very often. The Joads, on the other hand, fell apart like their car. As George Bluestone writes in a 1972 essay, although Ma Joad "savagely protests to the breakup of the family" (105), her protests do not stop Al, Connie, and Noah from leaving the fold. Another nail is struck into the family coffin when Ma appears to go "jackrabbit" (185) and even tells Pa to "drive on" (249) while she bumps along in the back of the car with Granma Joad's corpse. Whether because of poverty or insanity, the Joads cannot attain the winning power of family

Annotation
Admission of potential reader criticism
Summarizes Gish condition
Summarizes Joad condition; clarifies contrast
Second topic sentence
Begins details from Gish family
Identifies date of personal interview
Sets up contrast; gives details from literature
Present tense
Summarizes contrast

Gish 3

togetherness possessed by the Gishes. The cliché that blood is thicker than water must certainly be true, but in the Dust Bowl, blood satisfied no one's thirst.

> Transitional sentence

Some traits that might have seemed like advantages at the time of the Depression were ultimately insignificant. The fact that the Joads were white Anglo-Saxon Protestants, for example, did not help them in their time of need. Surprisingly, however, race did not adversely affect the Gishes. As Steinbeck's biographer Richard O'Conner claims, the white Joad family is forced to move after the "farm mortgage is forclosed, and they lose their land" (67). The implication in the historian William Katz's comments bears consideration: "There was not enough work" (24) even for white males. On the contrary, Grandfather Gish, whose father was biracial, went through the Depression as if it were nothing more than a rumor. At a time when, as the analyst Peter Lisca writes, "truth had run amuck, drunken upon prejudice" (79), no one gave any trouble to the Gishes or their farmland, which spanned nearly a hundred acres. The family was never rich, yet never poor. It was a respected family despite the mixed heritage, while the Joads were called "degenerate, sexual maniacs" (312) despite their place among the majority. Apparently, during the Great Depression, the color of someone's skin was not nearly as important as the color of money he could earn.

> Introduces third point; points out contrast

> In-text citation of author; only page reference needed

> Transitional phrase; introduces contrast

> Present tense

> Concluding sentence

Historians suggest that the Great Depression dramatically affected everyone, but some faced far more difficulties than

Gish 4

others. The Joads suffered greatly while the Gishes felt virtually
no effects. Several matters could give an edge over economic
despair, but the Joads knew none of them. Who was God in a
land where the Good Samaritan was an old wives' tale? What
was the use of keeping a family together if the members could
never agree? Even though they were "racially correct," the Joads
went wrong. The Depression was like a terrible game that truly
divided the economy's winners and losers.

> Conclusion emphasizes contrasts; asks questions with answers implied

> Concluding simile; reflects title

Gish 5

Works Cited

Bluestone, George. "The Grapes of Wrath." Steinbeck: A Collection

    of Critical Essays. Ed. Robert Murray Davis. Englewood

    Cliffs, NJ: Prentice Hall, 1972. 102–121.

Gish, James Owen. Personal interview. 23 December 1991.

Katz, William. An Album of the Great Depression. New York:

    Franklin Watts, 1978.

Lisca, Peter. "The Grapes of Wrath." Steinbeck: A Collection of

    Critical Essays. Ed. Robert Murray Davis. Englewood Cliffs,

    NJ: Prentice Hall, 1972. 75–101.

O'Conner, Richard. John Steinbeck. New York: McGraw-Hill, 1970.

Steinbeck, John. The Grapes of Wrath. 1939. New York: Penguin

    Books, 1979.

15

Analyzing a Science-Style Model

The humanities documentation style illustrated throughout this text is the most widely used form for research papers in humanities classes. It is not uncommon, however, for different schools, departments, and sometimes even individual instructors to require the science style of documentation. For this reason, this chapter illustrates Sarah's paper reformatted in science style.

SCIENCE-STYLE CITATIONS

Science-style citations are parenthetical; however, they include different information than do the humanities-style parenthetical citations. Note these distinctions:

1. All parenthetical citations include the author's name as well as the date of publication.

2. Page or paragraph numbers are included only if reference is made in the paper to a specific page, chapter, or section, or if a quotation is included.

3. When page numbers are included, they are preceded by the designation *p.* or *pp.*

4. When paragraph numbers are included (as for Web sites where no page number is available), they are preceded by the designation *para.*

5. Items in the citation are separated by commas.

Citations follow these general forms:

(Norvell, 2003)
(Norvell, 2003, p. 16)
(Norvell, 2003, pp. 16–17)

As in the humanities-style parenthetical citation, if the author's name appears in the text, it is not repeated in the parenthetical citation. Only the date and page reference appear in the note.

The Works Cited page is called the References page in science style, and it is also somewhat different from the humanities style. The most significant details are the following:

1. Only the author's initials appear for first and middle names.

2. The date of publication follows, parenthetically, the author's name.

3. Quotation marks are omitted from periodical article titles.

4. Only the first word and proper nouns of titles of books and periodical articles are capitalized. The first word of a subtitle is also capitalized.

5. For periodical titles, capitalize all words, except articles and prepositions (unless they are the first or last words).

6. Volume numbers of periodicals are underscored, or in italics, as your teacher directs.

7. Entries are double-spaced with hanging indentation, the second and subsequent lines indented.

Study the sample Reference pages in the model that follows, beginning on page 263.

Papers written in the science style are usually more technical than are those prepared in the humanities style. Often they report only primary research, and any references to secondary research are confined to introductory remarks in which the literature is summarized. Thus, the format closely resembles that of a technical report. Note the following details.

Title Page

The title page should be prepared according to the following specifications:

1. Arrange the title of the paper, the writer's name, and the writer's school affiliation centered left to right and top to bottom.

2. Double-space all parts, including any title that takes more than one line.

3. Place a running head, which is a shortened version of the title, at the top right margin, followed by five spaces and the page number 1.

Abstract

The abstract page, which summarizes the paper, follows the title page. It is always a single paragraph and should be 75–100 words for discussion, theory, or review papers and 100–150 words for experiment and observation papers. Use the following format for the abstract:

1. Place the running head flush right and a half inch from the top margin followed by the page number (2).

2. Center the title "Abstract" one inch from the top.

3. Begin the text a double space below the title.

4. Write the paragraph in block form, i.e., without the standard paragraph indentation.

Parts of the Paper

A paper written in science style often has multiple parts. Use the following guidelines to format the parts.

1. The first page of the paper repeats the title, centered, one inch from the top.

2. The text begins a double space below the title. An introduction, unlabeled, opens the paper by explaining the problem the research has examined. The remainder of the paper focuses on how the research was conducted and the results.

3. Use the same format to type headlines of the same level. Common headings that appear in science style papers include "Subjects,"

"Method," "Procedure," "Results," "Discussion," etc. Heads can also come directly from the outline.

4. Double-space tables, figures, and appendixes.

5. Put titles and labels at the top for tables and at the bottom for figures.

6. Place after the References page any appendixes providing statistical tables.

7. Begin each appendix on a new page and maintain the running head on pages numbered consecutively after the References page.

8. Center any titles, such as "Appendix A," one inch from the top of the page.

Study the following model pages.

Wetlands' Value   1

Running head
begins on
title page

Title of paper,
name, and school,
double-spaced,
centered left to
right and top
to bottom

Wetlands: Of What Value?

Sarah Blaser

West Terrace High School

Wetlands' Value 2

Abstract

Authorities do not necessarily agree on the definition of wetlands, and their disagreement has hindered thorough study of the habitat. Still, authorities agree that wetlands destruction has caused obvious environmental losses and continues to do so. The losses, caused primarily by uninformed human intervention, have resulted in seriously detrimental effects on plant and animal life, as well as on water storage, filtration, and storm runoff, a combination that ultimately affects the entire biosphere. When humans recognize the economic impact of wetlands losses, perhaps the loss can be stopped, if not reversed.

The word "Abstract" centered, double-spaced

Do not indent the first line of the paragraph

Abstract double-spaced, 75–100 words

Wetlands' Value 3

Wetlands: Of What Value?

Quaking bogs and snake-infested, mosquito-ridden swamps

make up the essence of chiller movies where the gooey slime

hides both crime and criminal, and the gloom is home to creepy

crawly things. These are wetlands. Is it any wonder that the

battle to save them—or what is left of them—has been so

difficult? When Earth's citizens recognize wetlands' value,

however, perhaps greater preservation measures will result.

At long last, wetlands are gaining respect as an integral part

of life's interdependence. Part of the problem, however, of

protecting wetlands is finding a definition everyone accepts. The

federally accepted standard was developed in 1979 by L. M.

Cowardin and three colleagues (31), who list five kinds of

wetlands: marine (formed by ocean tides), estuarine (formed by

salt water meeting fresh), lacustrine (formed by lakes), riverine

(formed along rivers and streams), and palustrine (formed as

marshes, swamps, and bogs). The current Environmental

Protection Agency (EPA) Web site designates four types:

marshes, swamps, bogs, and fens, with multiple subdivisions of

each (Values, 2003).

The terms categorizing wetlands, however, still do not

completely define them. As one writer explains the problem,

There is no generic swamp. Rather there are acid

swamps, cedar swamps, river swamps, bay swamps,

blackgum swamps and cypress swamps. There are fens

Running head
with page number
continues
throughout paper

All parts
double-spaced,
including title

Author name and
date included in
text; only page
number appears in
parenthetical note

Source named in
text; Web page
name differentiates
between two EPA
sources; no page
number needed

in Massachusetts, bogs in Maine, prairie potholes in the

Dakotas and sea grass beds and mangrove forests in

Florida. (Booth, 1990, p. 13)

To further complicate the problem of clear definition, wetlands

change, becoming marshes, wet meadows, eventually perhaps

shrub- or tree-filled swamps (Parrish, 2004). In addition, size

does not define a wetland. In fact, the most threatened wetlands

are not big or famous or maybe not even obvious, but instead are

"scattered tracts of private property you might drive right past"

(Easterbrook, 1989, p. 40).

The EPA, however, follows this general definition: Wetlands

are areas "where water covers the soil, or is present either at or

near the surface of the soil all year or for varying periods of time

during the year, including during the growing season" (Wetlands

types, 2003, para. 4). To put it plainly, if the soil is wet enough

often enough to affect the vegetation, the area is a wetland.

Depending on how one defines wetlands and depending on

whose statistics one reads, anywhere from half to two-thirds of

the United States' wetlands have been destroyed. In 1987 only

99 million acres remained, an area about the size of California,

less than half of the original wetland acreage. Most authorities

agree that the United States is losing 400,000 to 500,000 acres

of wetlands a year (Dahl, 2000, p. 3). For instance, wetlands

once covered 25% of Indiana; now the acreage is less than 4%

(Ind. DNR, 2004).

Page number required for direct quotation

Without direct quotation, only author and date needed

Author, date, and page cited for direct quotation

Source named in text; Web page title differentiates between two EPA sources; page number not available so paragraph number cited, required for direct quotation

Online publication; includes page number for specific statistics

E-mail citation; no page number needed

Wetlands' Value 5

The grievous losses are attributed to a number of factors. The National Wildlife Federation attributes 54% of loss to agriculture and 46% to development, including the following human activities that adversely affect wetlands: drainage, dredging and stream channelization, dumping fill material, diking and damming, grazing, tilling for crop production, building levees, logging, mining, introducing nonnative species, construction, and polluted runoff (2003). As long as humans continue these detrimental activities, wetlands will continue to disappear.

Given these vast losses, the real question for many is why should anyone care, especially when wetlands are "reviled as mosquito havens" (Youth, 2003, para. 1). As biological entities, however, wetlands improve water quality (acting as purifiers), recharge groundwater and reduce flooding (acting to retain water), and serve as habitat for half of the endangered and threatened species in the United States. They also contribute to biodiversity, fish and waterfowl habitat, and recreation (Ducks, 2002). Consequently, to destroy wetlands is to destroy a resource for plants and animals from the bottom of the food chain all the way up to humans.

Source named in text; only date required in citation

No page available on database; paragraph cited for quotation

No page or paragraph number required if not a direct quotation or statistics

Wetlands' Value 6

References

Booth, W. (1990, January 30). Rebuilding wetlands: Nature proves a tough act to follow. The Washington Post C13–14.

Cowardin, L. M., Carter, V., Golet, F. C., & LaRoe, E. T. (1979). Classification of wetlands and deepwater habitats of the United States. Washington, D.C.: US Fish and Wildlife Service.

Dahl, T. E. (2000). Status and trends of wetlands in the conterminous United States. National Wetlands Inventory. US Fish and Wildlife Service. Retrieved April 23, 2004, from http://wetlands.fws.gov/statusandtrends.htm.

Easterbrook, G. (1989, July 24). Cleaning up. Newsweek 138: 26, 42. Retrieved April 23, 2004, from Academic Search Elite Database.

Fullerton, J. (2003, March). Wetlands redefined again. Farm Journal 127: 28. Retrieved April 22, 2004, from MasterFILE Premier Database.

Goodwin, R. H., & Niering, W. A. (1975). Inland wetlands of the United States: Evaluated as potential registered natural landmarks. Washington, D.C.: GPO.

How much money is nature worth? (1997, August). Today's Science on File. Retrieved April 28, 2004, from Facts.com Database.

Indiana Department of Natural Resources Education Center. (2004, February 10). Wade into a wetland workshop. E-mail to the author.

Niering, W. A. (1985). Wetlands: The Audubon Society nature guides. New York: Alfred A. Knopf.

Parrish, F. K. (2004). Marsh. Encyclopedia Americana. Retrieved May 15, 2004, from http://go.grolier.com/.

Running head continues, double-spaced

"References" is centered, double-spaced

Hanging indentation

Title of article; only first and proper nouns capitalized

Title of Web site

Spell out names of months; year first, then month

Capitalize first word of subtitles

Omit angled brackets for Web addresses

Wetlands' Value 7

Poole, K. (2004, April 29). Personal interview.

Should nature have a price? (1997, August). <u>Today's Science on File</u>.
Retrieved April 28, 2004, from Facts.com Database.

Thompson, L. (2004, February 25). Cities weigh balance of nature.
<u>The Seattle Times</u> H10. Retrieved April 28, 2004, from
NewsBank Info Database.

Threats to wetlands. (2003). <u>National Wildlife Federation</u>. Retrieved
April 18, 2004, from http://nwf.org/wetlands/threats.html.

Values and functions of wetlands. (2003, January 17). United States
Environmental Protection Agency. Retrieved April 28, 2004,
from http://www.epa.gov/owow/wetlands/vital/what.html.

Wetland functions. (2002). <u>Conservation</u>. Ducks Unlimited, Inc.
Retrieved April 18, 2004, from http://www.ducks.org/
conservation/wetland_functions.asp.

Wetlands clean sewage the natural way. (1993, October). <u>Today's
Science on File</u>. Retrieved April 28, 2004, from Facts.com
Database.

Wetlands types. (2003, February 24). United States Environmental
Protection Agency. Retrieved April 28, 2004, from
http://www.epa.gov/owow/wetlands/types/.

Wolf-Armstrong, M. (2002). President's message. <u>Restore
America's Estuaries</u>. Retrieved April 28, 2004, from
http://www.estuaries.org/presidentmessage.php.

Youth, H. (2003, November). Winged messengers: Does habitat
loss signal biodiversity's death knell? <u>USA Today Magazine</u>.
Retrieved April 28, 2004, from MasterFILE Premier
Database.

Name of Web site identical to Web site sponsor; do not repeat

Two Web pages accessed from same Web site

Title of Web page followed by title of Web site, followed by name of Web site sponsor

Glossary

access refers to the ability to send or retrieve computerized information

bibliography a list of books and periodicals

bibliography card a card on which the bibliography information for a single source is recorded; includes title, author, and publishing information (See Chapter 5.)

body the paragraphs of a paper that develop the thesis; all except the introduction and conclusion (See Chapter 10.)

brackets the pair of punctuation marks [ ] in which a writer places explanatory words or phrases inside quoted material (See Chapter 7.)

catalog an alphabetically arranged system of indexing books in a library; includes access by subject, author, title, or keyword (See Chapter 3.)

CD-ROM an acronym that represents Compact Disk with Read-Only Memory, a laser disk on which can be stored vast amounts of material, such as an entire set of reference books

computer software any program that allows the computer to perform specific tasks, like word processing

conclusion the final paragraph of a paper in which the writer must leave readers satisfied that the thesis has been fully developed (See Chapter 10.)

cross-reference an indication, such as in an index listing, that more information will be found under another heading

database in computer language, a major collection of related data, such as a collection of hundreds of magazines or newspapers (See Chapter 3.)

Dewey decimal system one of two cataloging systems by which books are organized in libraries (Compare with *Library of Congress system*. See Chapter 3.)

documentation a means of crediting sources used in a research paper (See Chapters 12 and 15.)

drafting the process of writing the first copy of a paper (See Chapter 10.)

ellipses (i LIP seez) a series of spaced periods (...) showing the omission of words, phrases, or sentences from quoted material (See Chapter 7.)

file a set of data stored on a computer disk, CD, or external storage media

format the appearance, or layout, of the final manuscript, including details such as the placement of page numbers, size of margins, arrangement of long quotations, etc. (See Chapters 12 and 15.)

index an alphabetically arranged list of headings referring readers to specific pages (as an index in the back matter of a book) or to periodicals (as in an index online) (See Chapter 3.)

interview the process of talking with and questioning an authority on one's research topic in order to glean primary information to support the thesis (See Chapter 6.)

introduction in a paper, the opening paragraph in which the writer prepares the reader for the paper's contents by providing necessary background information, a thesis statement, and some technique by which to attract reader attention (See Chapter 10.)

Library of Congress system one of two cataloging systems by which books are organized in libraries (Compare with *Dewey decimal system*.) (See Chapter 3.)

modem (MOH dem) an acronym for MOdulator/DEModulator, the hardware that allows a computer user to access information through telephone lines

note, outline a note taken down in list or outline form as opposed to sentence form (See Chapter 7.)

note, paraphrase a note in which the researcher rewords and simplifies material but maintains about the same length as the source (See Chapter 7.)

note, partial quotation a note that includes some words or phrases quoted directly from the source, with quoted parts being enclosed in quotation marks (Compare with *note, quotation*.) (See Chapter 7.)

note, précis (pray SEE) a note taken in summary form (See Chapter 7.)

note, quotation a note made up of words, phrases, or sentences quoted from the source; a note enclosed entirely in quotation marks (Compare with *note, partial quotation*.) (See Chapter 7.)

note card a card on which a researcher records information found in primary or secondary sources, which is used to support the thesis of a research paper (See Chapter 7.)

objective refers to impartiality of a disinterested party (Compare with *subjective*.)

online refers to using the computer when it is connected to another computer, usually through a telecommunications network like telephone lines, satellites, and/or microwaves (See Chapter 3.)

online search a check of networked databases that can provide bibliography lists, abstracts, and/or complete articles suitable as research material (See Chapter 3.)

orphan a single line of the text of a paragraph that appears at the bottom of a page (Compare with *widow*.)

outline, working an informal outline that changes as a researcher works; guides selection of sources (See Chapter 2.)

pagination the use of consecutive numbers to indicate the order of pages in a paper

parenthetical documentation documentation placed inside parentheses within the text of the paper; credits sources of ideas and quotations appearing inside parentheses (See Chapter 12.)

plagiarism (PLAY juh riz um) using someone else's words or ideas without acknowledgment (See Chapter 7.)

prewriting the activities that prepare a writer for the actual drafting of the research paper, including choosing and narrowing a topic, searching for primary and secondary references, developing a working outline, taking notes, and preparing a final outline (See Chapters 1–9.)

primary sources references that are contemporary to a researcher's subject; firsthand materials, like a book, interview, survey response, letter, etc. (Compare with *secondary sources*.) (See Chapter 6.)

proofreading the process of checking a paper for grammar, mechanics, and usage (See Chapter 13.)

reference any print or nonprint media from which information is taken to develop a research paper

report a summary of information gleaned usually from a single source, such as an article, chapter, or book (See Chapter 1.)

research the process of gathering information to support a thesis (See Chapters 2–8.)

research paper, evaluative a paper that goes beyond a report, supports both a topic and a thesis, and gains a new point of view (See Chapter 1.)

research paper, factual a report gleaned from a series of resources (See Chapter 1.)

research question a paper's topic phrased as a question, which helps guide the research (See Chapters 1 and 9.)

revising the process of improving the text of the paper by checking content, organization, paragraph and sentence structure, and word choice (See Chapter 11.)

rough draft the first copy of text produced during the drafting process (See *drafting* and Chapter 10.)

scan to read quickly, looking for key words or ideas

secondary sources references that are secondhand, written later about someone or something (Compare with *primary sources*.) (See Chapter 3.)

slug the heading on a note card that corresponds to a heading on the working outline (See Chapter 7.)

source any print or nonprint medium from which information is taken to develop a research paper

statement of purpose a sentence that clarifies the reason for developing the thesis: to compare, to contrast, to explain, to persuade, to evaluate, to analyze, etc. (See Chapter 2.)

subjective referring to personal interests or biases; opposite of objective (See *objective*.)

subscription services paid services that provide libraries or other facilities access to databases; users typically need a password to use the services

survey a means of measuring response from a select group of people, the results of which are used as primary information to support a thesis (See Chapter 6.)

term paper a generic term that may refer to a report, a factual research paper, or an evaluative research paper (See *report*; *research paper, evaluative*; and *research paper, factual*.) (See also Chapter 1.)

thesis statement a statement that answers the research question, which guides the research (See Chapter 1) and indicates the precise contents of the paper (See Chapter 9.)

topic the narrowed subject of a paper (See Chapter 1.)

widow a single line of the text of a paragraph that appears at the top of a page (Compare with *orphan*.)

works cited page the page(s) at the end of a paper that lists alphabetically the sources from which the writer used information to develop the thesis (See Chapter 12.)

Index